LATIN AMERICAN POLITICAL, ECONOMIC, AND SECURITY ISSUES

ARGENTINA

CONDITIONS, ISSUES, AND U.S. RELATIONS

Latin American Political, Economic, and Security Issues

Additional books in this series can be found on Nova's website under the Series tab.

Additional e-books in this series can be found on Nova's website under the e-book tab.

LATIN AMERICAN POLITICAL, ECONOMIC, AND SECURITY ISSUES

ARGENTINA

CONDITIONS, ISSUES, AND U.S. RELATIONS

EILEEN MCKINNEY
EDITOR

nova publishers
New York

Library of Congress Cataloging-in-Publication Data

ISBN: 978-1-63482-251-0

Published by Nova Science Publishers, Inc. † New York

CONTENTS

PREFACE

This book discusses the conditions in Argentina as well as the issues and relations between Argentina and the United States.

Chapter 1 – Argentina, a South American country with a population of around 41 million, has had a vibrant democratic tradition since its military relinquished power in 1983. Current President Cristina Fernández de Kirchner, from a center-left faction of the Peronist party, was first elected in 2007 (succeeding her husband, Néstor Kirchner, who served one term) and is now approaching the final year of her second term. Argentina's constitution does not allow for more than two successive terms, so President Fernández is ineligible to run in the next presidential election, scheduled for October 2015. The presidential race is well underway with several candidates leading opinion polls, including two from the Peronist party. Argentina has Latin America's third-largest economy and is endowed with vast natural resources. Agriculture has traditionally been a main economic driver, but the country also has a diversified industrial base and a highly educated population. In 2001-2002, a severe economic crisis precipitated by unsustainable debt led to the government defaulting on nearly $100 billion in foreign debt owed to private creditors, the International Monetary Fund (IMF), and foreign governments. Subsequent Argentine administrations resolved more than 90% of the country's debt owed to private creditors through two debt restructurings offered in 2005 and 2010; repaid debt owed to the IMF in 2006; and, in May 2014, reached an agreement to repay foreign governments. Recent court rulings have increased pressure on Argentina to reach an agreement with private creditors who chose not to participate in the 2005 and 2010 debt restructuring offers. This outstanding debt has also prevented Argentina from accessing international credit markets, and could make it more difficult for Argentina to emerge from its current economic downturn. U.S.-Argentine relations, as described by the Department of State, are based on such shared interests as regional peace and stability, nuclear nonproliferation, human rights, education, and cooperation on science and technology. Commercial relations are robust, with the United States running a $5.7 billion trade surplus and U.S. companies investing approximately $15 billion in the country. At various junctures, however, there have been tensions in the bilateral relationship, including over Argentina's payment of international arbitral awards in investment disputes and the repayment of debt owed to the U.S. government. While these issues have been settled, the unresolved holdout debt issue has contributed to increased tension, with Argentine officials at times rhetorically lashing out at the United States. A continued interest of Congress is progress in the investigation and prosecution of those responsible for the 1994 bombing of the Argentine-Israeli Mutual Association (AMIA) that killed 85 people. Both Iran and Hezbollah are alleged to be linked to the bombing. This report provides background on the political and economic situation in Argentina and U.S.- Argentine relations. An appendix provides links to selected U.S. government reports on Argentina.

Chapter 2 – U.S.-Argentine economic relations have long history of mutually beneficial engagement. In recent years, however, they have been strained at times, in part because of Argentina's struggle to maintain macroeconomic stability, and also because of specific policy choices that have made the business environment difficult to navigate since the country's 2001 financial crisis. Following a steep currency devaluation and the largest sovereign default in history, Argentina entered a deep recession with high unemployment and social upheaval. It brought to power a new government, and with it a shift in economic policy away from market-oriented policies toward greater government control of the economy in pursuit of "social equity." The initial policy responses intended to restore order and address the most pressing social problems evolved into permanent social programs. Government policies introduced many distortions into the economy, including high inflation, which have required regular adjustments in the international accounts to maintain economic stability. These include managed trade, capital controls, and limited currency conversion, among other policies that have earned the ire of international stakeholders. Argentina's economic policies reflect priority for financial independence, social equity, and what may be considered a commitment to "populist" macroeconomic solutions. Even in recognizing that countries can govern themselves well under alternative policy frameworks, what stands out for many is the sense that Argentina's policy choices, with attendant economic distortions, increase the risk of a new financial crisis. The resulting spillovers into international economic policy are unavoidable. Trade protection, managed exchange rates, and capital controls, for example, are policy adjustments required to address problems that materialize in a constrained economic system (e.g., subsidy-driven fiscal expansion, price controls, inability to borrow internationally) that cannot easily accommodate current account deficits, a market exchange rate, or standard macroeconomic responses to high inflation. Congress and private U.S. stakeholders have opposed many of Argentina's policies that include a sovereign default on debt owed to both private investors and countries, including the United States; refusal to pay awards ordered by the International Centre for the Settlement of Investment Disputes (ICSID); nationalization of foreign assets; trade protectionism; capital and currency controls; and refusal to abide by International Monetary Fund (IMF) reporting requirements. Some U.S. investors are suing the government of Argentina in U.S. federal courts; the Obama Administration has invoked financial restrictions, revoked trade preferences, voted against loans for Argentina in the development banks, and filed cases before the World Trade Organization (WTO). Some Members of Congress have expressed dissatisfaction in hearings, resolutions, and proposed legislation. International stakeholders, both public and private, find themselves challenged by this system, along with some Argentines. One indication of the breadth of international dissatisfaction over Argentina's policies is the call for effectively removing Argentina from the G-20, despite the lack of precedent and formal procedure for doing so. Irrespective of these initiatives, Argentina has not been moved to change course, and Congress may decide to consider once again U.S. options for addressing bilateral concerns with Argentina.

Chapter 3 – Argentina is a federal constitutional republic. Cristina Fernandez de Kirchner won re-election to the presidency in October 2011 in multi-party elections the media and various nongovernmental organizations (NGOs) described as generally free and fair. The country also held legislative midterm elections on October 27. Security forces reported to civilian authorities but occasionally acted at lower levels independently of civilian control and committed human rights abuses. The principal human rights problems included reports of torture by provincial police, harsh prison conditions, and gender violence. Other human rights problems included use of excessive force by police; occasional arbitrary arrest and detention; prolonged pretrial detention; actions that risked impairing freedom of the press; continued concerns about judicial inefficiency; official corruption; child abuse; continuing discrimination against and infringements on the rights of indigenous people; sex trafficking; forced labor, primarily within the country;

and child labor. Judicial authorities prosecuted a number of officials who committed abuses during the year; however, some officials engaged in corruption or other abuses with impunity.

Chapter 4 – The constitution and other laws and policies protect religious freedom, and in practice, the government generally respected religious freedom. There were reports of societal discrimination based on religious affiliation, belief, or practice, including reports of anti-Semitism. U.S. embassy officers regularly discussed religious freedom with community leaders as well as the government. Embassy representatives attended events organized by religious groups that addressed religious freedom and promoted interfaith awareness and appreciation.

Chapter 5 – The Government of Argentina (GOA) took actions in the past year to improve the investment climate in Argentina. To regain investor confidence, the GOA settled outstanding international arbitral awards, engaged with the International Monetary Fund (IMF) to improve economic reporting data, and compensated the Spanish-firm Repsol for the partial expropriation of YPF in 2012. Argentina also engaged with the Paris Club group of creditors to address legacy debt issues. A January 2014 currency devaluation reduced costs and asset prices in dollar terms. Over the past year, one measure of Argentina's country risk has fallen approximately 35 percent from 1210 basis points to 790. The GOA has signaled its desire to see continued foreign direct investment (FDI) flows to enhance the nation's productive capacity and GDP growth potential. Although improved from the year before, investor confidence remains low. Longstanding concerns regarding the lack of transparency in government policymaking diminish the attractiveness of prospective investments in some sectors. Decisions that affect companies, both foreign and domestic, are frequently taken without industry input and rarely with a formal comment period. GOA actions to curb the remittance of profits abroad have also led some foreign companies to question whether their money should be invested in the country if they are unable to access it later. Currency controls delay companies' access to dollars to pay suppliers. The GOA's all-encompassing import licensing system has made it burdensome to import the materials necessary for the day-to-day functioning of a business. Factories and distributors occasionally sit idle while the GOA delays granting approval to move inputs through customs, a process that can be unpredictable. Companies that export more from Argentina than they import generally receive preferential access, but even these firms have reported difficulties in securing certain goods. Price controls have also caused difficulties for businesses. Argentina continues to owe debt to private bondholders. Ninety-two percent of the defaulted USD 82 billion of private debt has been swapped for a mix of new bonds with a substantial loss in net present value. Some bondholders, known as the "holdouts," have not participated in the swaps and continue to pressure Argentina via the U.S. courts to settle its outstanding debt for the actual amount they are owed plus interest. Argentina's growth slowed in 2013 to 3 percent and unemployment remained steady at 6.4 percent, according to official figures. Central Bank reserves dipped to USD 27 billion down from their high of USD 52 billion in early 2011. This decline has been due to reserves having been used to service debt, maintain the exchange rate, and meet other balance of payment needs. The 2014 budget allowed the use of USD 9.8 billion in Central Bank reserves to make debt payments. Argentina ran current and financial account deficits in 2013 that also contributed to a decline in reserves. After several years of publishing non-credible statistics, Argentina's official statistics agency (INDEC) released substantially revised inflation and GDP growth data that are closer in line with private estimates. The IMF had formally censured Argentina in February 2013 because of manipulation of inflation and GDP data, a breach of obligation to the Fund under the Articles of Agreement. As of publication of this report, the IMF had not yet released its conclusions regarding its review of Argentina's new data.

In: Argentina
Editor: Eileen Mckinney

ISBN: 978-1-63482-251-0

Chapter 1

ARGENTINA: BACKGROUND AND U.S. RELATIONS*

Mark P. Sullivan and Rebecca M. Nelson

SUMMARY

Argentina, a South American country with a population of around 41 million, has had a vibrant democratic tradition since its military relinquished power in 1983. Current President Cristina Fernández de Kirchner, from a center-left faction of the Peronist party, was first elected in 2007 (succeeding her husband, Néstor Kirchner, who served one term) and is now approaching the final year of her second term. Argentina's constitution does not allow for more than two successive terms, so President Fernández is ineligible to run in the next presidential election, scheduled for October 2015. The presidential race is well underway with several candidates leading opinion polls, including two from the Peronist party.

Argentina has Latin America's third-largest economy and is endowed with vast natural resources. Agriculture has traditionally been a main economic driver, but the country also has a diversified industrial base and a highly educated population. In 2001-2002, a severe economic crisis precipitated by unsustainable debt led to the government defaulting on nearly $100 billion in foreign debt owed to private creditors, the

* This is an edited, reformatted and augmented version of a Congressional Research Service publication R43816, prepared for Members and Committees of Congress, dated December 9, 2014.

International Monetary Fund (IMF), and foreign governments. Subsequent Argentine administrations resolved more than 90% of the country's debt owed to private creditors through two debt restructurings offered in 2005 and 2010; repaid debt owed to the IMF in 2006; and, in May 2014, reached an agreement to repay foreign governments. Recent court rulings have increased pressure on Argentina to reach an agreement with private creditors who chose not to participate in the 2005 and 2010 debt restructuring offers. This outstanding debt has also prevented Argentina from accessing international credit markets, and could make it more difficult for Argentina to emerge from its current economic downturn.

U.S.-Argentine relations, as described by the Department of State, are based on such shared interests as regional peace and stability, nuclear nonproliferation, human rights, education, and cooperation on science and technology. Commercial relations are robust, with the United States running a $5.7 billion trade surplus and U.S. companies investing approximately $15 billion in the country. At various junctures, however, there have been tensions in the bilateral relationship, including over Argentina's payment of international arbitral awards in investment disputes and the repayment of debt owed to the U.S. government. While these issues have been settled, the unresolved holdout debt issue has contributed to increased tension, with Argentine officials at times rhetorically lashing out at the United States. A continued interest of Congress is progress in the investigation and prosecution of those responsible for the 1994 bombing of the Argentine-Israeli Mutual Association (AMIA) that killed 85 people. Both Iran and Hezbollah are alleged to be linked to the bombing.

This report provides background on the political and economic situation in Argentina and U.S.- Argentine relations. An appendix provides links to selected U.S. government reports on Argentina.

Political and Economic Situation

In December 2013, Argentina—a South American nation located in the continent's southern cone—celebrated 30 years of civilian democratic rule since the military relinquished power after 7 years of harsh dictatorship. The military's so-called Dirty War against leftists and their sympathizers in the late 1970s and early 1980s had resulted in thousands of disappearances. The military ultimately fell into disrepute in the aftermath of its failure in the Falkland Islands (Islas Malvinas) war with Great Britain in 1982, and the country returned to civilian democratic rule with the election of Raúl Alfonsín of the Radical Civic Union (UCR) as president in 1983.

Argentina at a Glance

Population: 41.45 million (2013, WB).

Area: 1.1 million square miles, about the size of the United States east of the Mississippi; second-largest country in South America and eighth-largest country in the world.

GDP: $610.3 billion (2013, current prices, IMF).

Per Capita GDP: $14,709 (2013, current prices, IMF est.)

Key Trading Partners: Brazil (24%), China (11%), United States (8%) (2013, INDEC).

Life Expectancy: 76 (2012, WB) Literacy: 98% (2011, WB)

Legislature: Bicameral Congress, with 72-member Senate and 257-member Chamber of Deputies.

Sources: International Monetary Fund (IMF); National Institute of Statistics and Census, INDEC (Argentina); World Bank (WB); and U.S. Department of State.

Carlos Menem of the Justicialist Party (PJ), also known as the Peronist Party, won the 1989 elections and served two presidential terms until 1999, during which he transformed Argentina from having a state-dominated protectionist economy to one committed to free market principles and open to trade.[1] Increasing corruption and high unemployment, however, led to the defeat of the Peronists in the 1999 presidential election, which was won by Fernando de la Rúa of the UCR as the candidate of a coalition known as the Alliance for Work, Justice, and Education.

In 2001-2002, Argentina's democratic political system endured considerable stress amid a severe economic crisis and related social unrest. In late 2001, as the banking system faltered and confidence in the government of President de la Rúa evaporated, widespread demonstrations turned violent, and the President resigned. The subsequent interim government then defaulted on nearly $100 billion in public debt, the largest sovereign default in history at the time. Ultimately, the political system survived the crisis. President Eduardo Duhalde (January 2002-May 2003), a Peronist (Justicialist Party, PJ) Senator selected by Congress to fill out the remainder of President de la Rúa's term, implemented policies that stabilized the economy; then, left-leaning President Néstor Kirchner (May 2003-December 2007), a Peronist who had served as a provincial governor of Santa Cruz in Patagonia, further enhanced internal political and economic stability.

Source: Prepared by Calvin C. DeSouza, Geospatial Information Systems Analyst, CRS.

Figure 1. Map of Argentina, with Provinces.

Despite some difficulties, Kirchner made popular policy moves in the areas of human rights and economic policy that helped restore Argentines' faith in democracy. In June 2005, the government offered the first of two restructurings of its defaulted private bond debt with a historically low recovery rate to bondholders (about 30% on a net present value basis). While this was politically popular in Argentina, the government's failure to repay its arrears to official Paris Club creditors or to reach a deal with remaining private creditors in defaulted bond debt who did not accept the government's offer continued to prevent Argentina from having full access to international capital markets. Legislative elections in 2005 demonstrated strong support for Kirchner; his left-leaning wing of the PJ, known as the Front for Victory (FPV), made significant gains. Kirchner would have been eligible to run again in the 2007 presidential elections, but instead he supported the candidacy of his wife, Senator Cristina Fernández de Kirchner (hereinafter Fernández).

Cristina Fernández is now in her second term as president. She won the 2007 presidential election with 45% of the vote, defeating her closest rival by 23 points, and became the first woman in Argentine history to be elected president. In concurrent legislative elections, Fernández's FPV faction of the PJ gained further seats, solidifying its majority in both houses of Argentina's bicameral Congress. Nevertheless, Fernández's political honeymoon was short-lived because of an energy crisis and a series of farmers' strikes that led to the congressional defeat of her proposed tax increase on key agricultural exports. As a result, the Kirchners suffered a significant setback in the 2009 legislative elections, with the FPV losing control of both houses. It appeared that former President Kirchner was poised to run again for the presidency in 2011, but his death from a heart attack changed the political landscape. Instead, Fernández ran for reelection and won a second mandate in October 2011 with 54% of the vote, the largest percentage in a presidential race since the country's return to democratic rule. Her support was buoyed by an outpouring of sympathy after the death of her husband as well as by the absence of a strong opposition candidate. The President's FPV also regained a legislative majority in both houses of Congress.

President Fernández's popularity, however, fell considerably after her reelection amid large-scale public protests against corruption, increasing crime, the government's economic policies and the government's efforts to exert influence over the media and the judiciary. In Argentina's October 2013 legislative elections, in which one-half of the Chamber of Deputies and one-third of the Senate were at stake, President Fernández's Front for Victory managed to retain control of both houses. The FPV and its allies gained several seats in the 257-seat Chamber of Deputies, and in the 72-member Senate, the FPV lost several seats, but retained a majority.[2] Nevertheless, the

FPV was unable to secure the two-thirds majorities needed to approve a constitutional reform that would have allowed President Fernández to run for a third consecutive term in 2015.

October 2015 Presidential Election[3]

Argentina's next presidential election is scheduled for October 25, 2015; a second round will be held between the two leading candidates on November 24 if no candidate in the first round receives more than 45% of the vote, or, if receiving more than 40% of the vote, fails to achieve a 10-point lead over the next candidate. The deadline for presenting electoral alliances among the political parties is June 10, and a primary is scheduled for August 9, 2015, for all of the alliances.[4]

The presidential race is already underway, with four contenders topping opinion polls at this juncture. The 2013 legislative elections raised the profile of a centrist dissident Peronist faction known as the Renewal Front (FR) led by *Sergio Massa* (a former Fernández cabinet chief and former mayor of Tigre) who was elected to the Chamber of Deputies. Massa reportedly is now one of the leading candidates in the presidential race. At 42 years of age, Massa reportedly represents a generation of young politicians with experience in government and a reputation as an efficient administrator. He served as head of Argentina's National Social Security Administration (ANES) from 2002 to 2007 under Presidents Duhalde and Kirchner. Massa is garnering support from Peronists disillusioned with the Fernández government.

Another leading Peronist candidate for the presidency is *Daniel Scioli*, the governor of Buenos Aires province. Scioli, a close ally of President Kirchner, served as his Vice President from 2003 to 2007. While he remains a part of President Fernández's Front for Victory faction of the Peronist party, he reportedly is not close to Fernández. As a potential candidate of the FPV, Scioli would benefit from Fernández's continued popular support—in early November 2014, polls showed the President with relatively high approval ratings of between 40% and 47%.[5] While currently strong in the polls, Scioli's presidential prospects could diminish if President Fernández chooses to endorse another Peronist candidate.

A third leading candidate for the presidency is *Mauricio Macri*, the leader of the center-right *Propuesta Republicana* (PRO, Republican Proposal) party who is in his second term as mayor of Buenos Aires. One difficulty for his candidacy is that his political party is centered in Buenos Aires and does not have a nationwide reach, so it is likely that he would need to form a coalition with other parties in order to be elected. In September 2014, an electoral alliance between Macri's PRO and the center-left UCR won the mayoralty of a small town in Córdoba province in central Argentina. Some observers maintain the victory could portend a national PRO-UCR alliance for the presidential race, while others believe it is more likely that the UCR will seek to join a center-left alliance for the election.[6]

Another potential candidate from outside Peronism is *Hermes Binner*, the leader of the center-left *Partido Socialista* (PS). Binner placed second in the 2011 presidential election as the candidate of the Broad Progressive Front coalition, receiving almost 17% of the vote. He served as governor of Santa Fe province from 2007 to 2011, and previously had served as mayor of Rosario, Argentina's third-largest city. Binner, who reportedly has an image as an honest politician, could play a role in the 2015 elections as the potential candidate of a center-left alliance of parties known as the Broad Front UNEN (Unity and Meeting) established in April 2014.

For over a decade, opposition parties have not been able to gain nationwide support to win the presidency. Many analysts contend, therefore, that it is likely that a Peronist candidate will succeed Fernández. Some analysts speculate, however, that it is likely that a second round of voting will be needed and that a non-Peronist candidate could capture the presidency in such a scenario.

Some observers venture that President Fernández may even seek a legislative seat in 2015 (or potentially a seat in the Parliament of Mercosur [Common Market of the South], also known as Parlasur) as a way to preserve her political influence after her presidency and possibly position herself to vie for a third presidential term in 2019.[7] (At the same time as the presidential race in October 2015, Argentina will hold elections for one-half of the Chamber of Deputies and one-third of the Senate as well as seats for Parlasur.) If a Peronist does not win the presidency, Fernández would be in a good position to play a key role in the Peronist party, particularly since the FPV will continue to have significant representation in Congress. If a Peronist wins, however, it could prove more difficult for Fernández to retain her political influence.

Human Rights Issues

Both the Kirchner and the Fernández governments have made significant efforts to bring to justice those responsible for the killing of thousands of people (some 30,000, according to Argentine human rights groups)[8] and the torture of thousands during the Dirty War, which occurred under military rule from 1976 to 1983. Since the Argentine Supreme Court overturned amnesty laws in 2003, more than 400 people, including many former military and police officials, have been convicted for the atrocities committed under military rule. These have included former military rulers General Jorge Rafael Videla (1976-1981), who died in prison in 2013, and General Reynaldo Bignone (1982-1983), who remains in prison. Argentine judicial authorities also continue to investigate cases of kidnapping and the illegal adoption of children born to those detained under the dictatorship.[9]

Despite progress in addressing past abuses, some human rights groups have criticized the current Argentine government regarding press freedom as well as alleged efforts to thwart judicial independence. Press rights groups have criticized the government for punishing media outlets critical of the government by withholding public advertising and instead awarding such advertising to outlets close to the government.

Over the past several years, the government has battled with the Clarín media group, which owns Argentina's most widely read newspaper, as well as radio stations, broadcast and cable television outlets, and an Internet service provider. In 2009, the government enacted a controversial law regulating broadcast and print media which it indicated was designed to strengthen pluralism and information freedom. The government maintained that it wanted Clarín to sell some of its assets in order to create more competition in the media market, while some press rights groups contended that the government actually wanted to muzzle Clarín, which has often been critical of the government. In October 2013, Argentina's Supreme Court upheld key provisions of the law. Clarín subsequently presented a plan to the government to break up its holdings into six different companies. An outline of the plan initially had been approved by the government's regulatory agency, the Federal Audiovisual Communications Authority (AFSCA) in February 2014, but in October 2014, the board of directors of AFSCA voted against Clarín's plan and said that the agency itself would undertake enforcement of the media law and the breakup of the media group.

The President of the AFSCA said that Clarín's plan would have maintained linkages among the new companies and violated the spirit of the media law.[10]

In April 2013, President Fernández pushed a series of bills through Congress that were designed to reform Argentina's judicial system. The most controversial of these reforms would have expanded the council of magistrates (the body which oversees the judiciary) with several members elected by popular vote. Opposition groups strongly criticized the judicial reform as a means to exert further influence over the judicial branch and for attempting to politicize it. In June 2013, Argentina's Supreme Court struck down the controversial provision requiring the election of magistrates, dealing a significant political blow to the Fernández government.

Economic Snapshot and Challenges

With a gross domestic product (GDP) of $610 billion (2013, IMF), Argentina has the third-largest economy in Latin America after Brazil and Mexico. The country has vast natural resources, including abundant fertile land suitable for agriculture, which have traditionally been the main drivers of economic growth. A highly educated population and a diversified industrial base also contribute to growth. Argentina is classified by the World Bank as an upper-middle-income developing economy.[11] Poverty rates, which had increased a decade ago because of the 2001- 2002 financial crisis, have fallen considerably in recent years as the economy has recovered. In 2012, Argentina's urban poverty rate was 4.3% compared to 30.6% in 2005.[12]

The global economic recession in 2009 had a negative effect on the Argentine economy, which contracted slightly by 0.1%. The economy rebounded in 2010 and 2011, however, with growth averaging 8.8%, due to an improvement in the global economy and higher demand for Argentina's exports by China (especially soybeans) and Brazil (especially cars and other vehicles). Argentina's economic growth slowed considerably in 2012 to an estimated 0.9% due to a variety of factors. These include sluggish global demand, high inflation, and a drought that affected agricultural production. Growth was also dampened by domestic economic policies, such as import and foreign currency controls, that discouraged foreign investment and made it more difficult for businesses to acquire capital goods. In 2013, a strong agricultural harvest resulted in an estimated growth rate of 2.9%.[13]

This year, however, the economy entered into a recession. While Argentine Minister of Economy and Public Finance Axel Kicillof maintains that growth resumed in the second quarter of 2014, and forecasts a growth rate of 0.5% for the year, the IMF and private economists are skeptical. The International Monetary Fund (IMF) forecasts that the Argentine economy will contract 1.7% in 2014 and 1.5% in 2015 because of macroeconomic imbalances and uncertainties related to the standoff with holdout creditors.[14] The Economist

Intelligence Unit (EIU) forecasts an economic contraction of 0.6% for 2014 and only a modest increase of 0.3% in 2015, and has expressed concerns about the accuracy of Argentina's official statistics.[15]

There are also some concerns that Argentina's economic deterioration could threaten some of the social gains that the country has made over the past decade.[16] In order to assist the Argentine government in this area, the World Bank approved a new three-year program in September 2014, with funding approaching $3 billion to support poverty reduction and inclusive growth in Argentina.[17]

The Argentine government has consistently understated inflation since 2007. In February 2014, the government took action to improve its reporting on inflation and unveiled a new consumer price index, but private economists remain skeptical. Private economists estimate that inflation in 2014 was running at more than 40% by October.[18]

At this juncture, a significant economic challenge for the Fernández government is how to resolve its outstanding defaulted external debt owed to remaining private creditors (approximately $15 billion, with principal and past due interest) who did not participate in Argentina's 2005 and 2010 bond exchanges (also see "Debt Issues" below). The outstanding debt has effectively blocked Argentina from the international credit markets. On a positive note, Argentina reached an agreement with the Paris Club group of official creditors in May 2014 to repay some $9.7 billion (including $608 million owed to the U.S. government) over a five-year period; it made its first Paris Club payment in late July 2014, with the next payment due in May 2015.[19] Yet the ongoing conflict with private creditors has essentially counteracted the positive effects of Argentina's agreement to resolve debt to official bilateral creditors and could increase the risk of a balance of payments crisis.[20]

U.S.-ARGENTINE RELATIONS

Overview

In the aftermath of Argentina's return to democracy in 1983, the United States and Argentina developed strong relations, which were especially close during the presidency of Carlos Menem (1989-1999). At times, however, there have been tensions in the bilateral relationship. The tough U.S. approach toward Argentina during its political and financial crisis in 2001-2002, in which the United States supported the cutoff of assistance from the IMF until Argentina committed to a sustainable economic plan, caused friction. Today, the State Department maintains that bilateral relations are based on such shared interests as regional peace and stability, nonproliferation, human rights, education, cultural exchanges, commercial ties, and cooperation on science and technology initiatives.[21] U.S. officials commend Argentina's contributions to international peacekeeping operations; currently Argentina contributes almost 900 military troops and police to operations worldwide. Because of these contributions, the United States designated Argentina as a major non-NATO ally in 1997. Argentina has not traditionally received much U.S. foreign assistance because of its relatively high per capita income, but in recent years it has received small amounts of assistance for military education and training and assistance to enhance its strategic trade control compliance and enforcement. An estimated $590,000 was provided to Argentina in FY2014, and the Administration requested the same amount for FY2015.

Tensions in bilateral relations increased in 2011 because of two incidents that occurred in the aftermath of a White House decision to exclude a visit to Argentina on President Obama's first trip to South America. First, Argentine Foreign Minister Hector Timerman criticized the decision of the mayor of Buenos Aires to send two police officials to the U.S.-backed International Law Enforcement Academy in El Salvador, which provides police management and specialized training to officials from throughout Latin America. Timerman publicly suggested that the school was teaching oppressive tactics. In another incident in 2011, Argentine officials seized U.S. government equipment associated with joint training activities on hostage rescue and crisis management between U.S. military personnel and Argentine federal police. According to the Department of State, the training had been approved by Argentine officials and the equipment involved was standard gear associated with the training.[22] Foreign Minister Timerman supervised the seizure of the cargo at the airport (opening part of the cargo in front of the press), which according to U.S. officials, was coordinated at the highest levels of the Argentine government.[23] Ultimately, tensions waned after an Argentine court ruled that the incident was not a criminal case, but a problem with customs clearance.

With regard to U.S.-Argentine commercial relations, the United States ran a $5.7 billion trade surplus with Argentina in 2013, exporting $10.3 billion in goods to the country (led by oil and machinery) and importing about $4.6 billion in goods (led by crude oil). In 2013, Argentina was the 31st-largest export market for the United States. For Argentina, the United States was its third-largest trading partner (after Brazil and China) in 2013, with imports from the United States accounting for almost 11% of its total imports and exports to the United States accounting for about 5% of its total exports.[24] According to the U.S. Trade Representative's 2014 *National Trade Estimate Report on Foreign Trade Barriers*, Argentina imposes a growing number of customs and licensing procedures and requirements that makes importing U.S. products more difficult. In August 2014, a World Trade Organization (WTO) dispute settlement panel ruled that Argentina's import license restrictions violated WTO rules. The case had been initiated by the United States, the European Union, and Japan.[25]

The stock of U.S. foreign direct investment in Argentina amounted to $15.2 billion in 2013 (up from $14.6 billion in 2012), concentrated in manufacturing and nonbanking holding companies.[26] Over 500 U.S. companies have invested in the country; in July 2013, Chevron announced that it would invest $1.24 billion in the development of the Vaca Muerta shale oil and gas field in Neuquén province in southwest Argentina.

While the United States and Argentina have a bilateral investment treaty in place, Argentina has taken actions in recent years that have dampened the investment climate. Over the past year, however, the government of President Cristina Fernández has taken several positive measures. These include settling several outstanding international arbitral awards (including, in October 2013, almost $300 million owed to three U.S. companies in cases that had been brought to the International Centre for the Settlement of Investment Disputes [ICSID, a branch of the World Bank Group]);[27] engaging with the IMF to improve the country's reporting of its economic growth and inflation data; and, as noted above and discussed in more detail below, reaching an agreement with the Paris Club group of official creditors in May 2014 to repay its overdue debt.

Despite these actions, the Department of State maintains that investor confidence in the country remains low because of long-standing concerns regarding the lack of transparency in government policymaking; efforts by the government to curb the remittance of profits abroad; currency controls that delay companies' access to dollars to pay suppliers; and a comprehensive import licensing system that makes it difficult to import materials for businesses.[28] Argentina also has been on the U.S. Trade Representative's Special 301 Priority Watch List since 1996 because of problems with intellectual property rights enforcement; USTR's 2014 report maintains that Argentina made little progress in this area over the past year, and noted particular concern over high levels of piracy and counterfeiting and the lack of political will to address the situation.[29]

Assistant Secretary of State for Western Hemisphere Affairs Roberta Jacobson acknowledged in September 2014 that U.S.-Argentine relations "are in a tough period right now." She maintained that the litigation involving private creditors is an issue for the courts to decide, but expressed hope "that it can be resolved in a way that Argentina can return to the international community, that Argentina can begin to grow and be productive again."[30] Argentine officials, likely attempting to play to a domestic audience, have lashed out at the United States regarding the debt issue. The Chargé d'Affaires at the U.S. Embassy in Argentina, Kevin Sullivan, made comments to the Argentine press in September 2014 in which he stated that "it is important for Argentina to emerge from default as soon as possible to return to the path of sustainable economic growth and attract the investment it needs." Both Foreign Minister Timerman and President Fernández condemned the U.S. diplomat's comments as an intrusion into Argentina's internal affairs.[31] President Fernández also asserted in a speech on September 30, 2014, that "if anything happens to me ... look North," referring to the United States, and alleged that economic sectors in Argentina wanted to oust her government with outside help.[32]

Debt Issues[33]

Argentina's default in 2001 has been a long-standing issue in relations with the United States. Argentina faced an acute economic crisis in 2001 that led to its default on nearly $100 billion of debt: $81.8 billion owed to private creditors; $6.3 billion owed to other governments, including the United States; and $9.5 billion owed to the IMF.[34] Reaching a resolution to the government's default has been a complex process that has taken more than a decade, and some issues still remain outstanding. In terms of debt owed to official creditors (other governments and international organizations), Argentina repaid the IMF in full in 2006, but only reached an agreement to repay other governments in May 2014. In terms of debt owed to private creditors, Argentina restructured more than 90% of the debt owed to private bondholders. It has faced legal challenges from the remaining bondholders—the "holdouts." Recent court rulings have favored the holdouts, but Argentina remains in default on this debt.

Debt Owed to the Paris Club Countries

After more than a decade, Argentina took steps in 2014 to resolve its default on debt owed to the "Paris Club" countries. The Paris Club is a voluntary, informal group of creditor governments, including the United States, that negotiates and/or reduces debt owed to them by other countries on a case-by-case basis.[35] After defaulting on its Paris Club debt in 2001, Argentina negotiated with the Paris Club in 2008 and 2010, but the parties failed to reach an agreement in these talks.

As economic conditions in Argentina became more difficult, including being cut off from international capital markets and facing a shortage of foreign currencies (particularly dollars), Argentina again approached the Paris Club countries in January 2014 with a proposal for repaying its debts to these governments.[36] In May 2014, a multilateral agreement was reached between the Argentine government and the Paris Club countries that set out repayment terms for the amount outstanding, which had grown to $9.7 billion including the principal and accrued interest, including $608 million to the United States.[37] In addition to the United States, Argentina owes money to Germany and Japan, which together account for more than half of Argentina's Paris Club debt, as well as the Netherlands, Spain, Italy, and Switzerland.[38] Markets responded positively to the announcement of the agreement.[39] Argentina made its first payment of $650 million under the agreement in July 2014. The next payment, of $550 million, is due in May 2015.

Although Argentina has made payments under the Paris Club agreement, formal implementation of the agreement requires signed bilateral agreements between Argentina and Paris Club members. This process is currently in progress. When the bilateral agreement with the United States is finalized, Argentina will no longer be in default on debt owed to the U.S. government. Restrictions in the Foreign Assistance Act of 1961 (Section 620(q)) prohibiting aid to countries in default to the U.S. government would be lifted.

Debt Owed to Private Bondholders

Argentina remains in default on a portion of its private sector debt, and recent court rulings have increased pressure on Argentina to reach an agreement with private creditors on this debt. Most of the defaulted debt held by private creditors was resolved through bond exchanges offered by the Argentine government in 2005 and, again, in 2010. In the exchanges, the Argentine government extended a unilateral offer to private bondholders to exchange the defaulted bonds for new bonds at a steep loss (approximately a net present value loss of 70%). Although the terms were widely viewed as unfavorable for the bondholders, more than 90% of bondholders agreed to participate in the exchanges. Until recently, investors holding the restructured Argentine bonds had received the full payments due on these bonds. Issues have arisen with recent payments, discussed below.

A small group of private investors—the holdouts—did not participate in the exchanges and have not received any payment from Argentina since the 2001 default. They are now owed approximately $15 billion, including principal and past due interest. Most of the holdouts are hedge funds that bought the bonds in secondary markets at steep discounts after the default. The holdouts have pursued litigation to seek full repayment from Argentina, primarily in the United States, since a large proportion of Argentine bonds were issued under New York law.

Although the legal cases have examined a number of issues, the most consequential ruling relates to the interpretation of a clause in the bond contracts that dictates creditors be treated equally: the "pari passu" clause. A smaller group of the holdout creditors, with claims totaling $1.3 billion, argue that paying the exchange bondholders while repudiating the holdout bonds is a breach of this provision. In 2012, a New York federal district court judge, Thomas Griesa, ruled in favor of the holdouts. As a result, if Argentina does not pay the group of litigating holdouts, U.S. financial institutions legally cannot transfer interest payments from Argentina to the exchange bondholders.[40] In effect, for Argentina to pay the exchange bondholders, it would have to pay the holdouts as well. The ruling was appealed, eventually reaching the Supreme Court. The Supreme Court announced in June 2014 that it would not hear the case, letting the previous ruling stand.

Following the Supreme Court announcement, the Argentine government faced a difficult decision. It could either (a) pay the holdouts and the exchange bondholders or (b) pay neither group, and default on its debt. On one hand, paying the holdouts would be financially and politically costly. Financially, the court ruling involved only a small group of holdouts, with a claim totaling $1.3 billion. However, other holdouts are also now pursuing similar legal recourse to the initial group that went to court over the "pari parssu" clause.[41] Argentina reportedly estimates that paying all remaining holdout creditors would cost $15 billion.[42] Politically, paying the holdouts could be seen as the Argentine government "caving" to foreign investors, and some analysts argue that President Fernández has "staked her political career on fighting the holdouts."[43] On the other hand, defaulting on its debt would make it difficult for Argentina to regain access to international capital markets, which many economists believe is critical for helping the struggling economy.

Last-minute negotiations between Argentina and holdout bondholders failed to reach a settlement. Argentina was facing a payment on the exchange bonds on July 30, 2014. Argentina transferred the funds to an intermediary bank (the Bank of New York Mellon), but did not pay the holdouts. Legally, the intermediary bank could not transfer the funds to the exchange bondholders, and on July 30, 2014, the credit rating agency Standard and Poor's declared Argentina to be in default, for the eighth time in Argentina's history. Argentine officials argue that because it transferred the funds, it should not count as a "default."[44]

The Argentine government has indicated it may be willing to negotiate with creditors in 2015, after a clause in the exchange bonds expires at the end of 2014. This clause forbids Argentina from voluntarily offering a better deal to the holdouts than it gave in the 2005 and 2010 exchanges without extending the same deal to all creditors.[45] In the meantime, Argentina has attempted to circumvent its dilemma by devising a new bond swap that would offer the holders of Argentine bonds issued under New York jurisdiction the opportunity to exchange them for new bonds under Argentine or French jurisdiction.[46] In response, on September 29, 2014, the New York federal district court judge in the case held Argentina in contempt of court, and warned that it would suffer repercussions if it defied his order regarding payment to bondholders.[47]

While the full ramifications of the recent developments remain to be seen, some analysts believe that they could undermine progress that Argentina had made in 2013 and the first half of 2014 to repair its decade-long "rogue debtor" reputation and normalize its status in the international economy. In addition to reaching an agreement with the Paris Club, Argentina agreed to settle several international investment disputes that had been brought to the ICSID, including, as noted above, several disputes with U.S. companies, while in February 2014 it agreed to a $5 billion settlement with Repsol, a Spanish oil firm, ending a two-year dispute over Argentina's expropriation of the company's operations.

AMIA Investigation

Congress has expressed concern over the years about progress into the investigation of the July 1994 bombing in Buenos Aires of the Argentine-

Israeli Mutual Association (AMIA) that killed 85 people. Both Iran and Hezbollah (the radical Lebanon-based Islamic group with strong ties to Iran) are alleged to be linked to the AMIA bombing as well as to the 1992 bombing of the Israeli Embassy that killed 30 people.

In 2004, Argentine Special Prosecutor Alberto Nisman was appointed to lead the AMIA investigation. Until then, progress on the investigation and prosecution of those responsible for the 1994 bombing had been stymied because of the government's mishandling of the case. In September 2004, a three-judge panel acquitted all 22 Argentine defendants in the case and faulted the shortcomings of the original investigation. With Nisman's appointment in 2004, however, the government moved forward with a new investigation. As a result, an Argentine judge issued arrest warrants in November 2006 for nine foreign individuals: an internationally wanted Hezbollah militant from Lebanon, Imad Mughniyah (subsequently killed by a car bomb in Damascus, Syria, in 2008), and eight Iranian government officials.

INTERPOL, the International Criminal Police Organization, subsequently posted Red Notices (international wanted persons notices) in 2007 for Mughniyah and five of the Iranian officials: Ali Fallahijan (former Iranian intelligence minister, 1989-1997); Mohsen Rabbani (former Iranian cultural attaché at the Iranian Embassy in Buenos Aires); Ahmad Reza Asghari (former third secretary at the Iranian Embassy in Buenos Aires); Ahmad Vahidi (who served as Iran's defense minister from 2009 to 2013); and Mohsen Rezai (former commander of Iran's Islamic Revolutionary Guard Corps, 1981-1997, and two-time presidential candidate).[48] In 2009, Argentina also issued an arrest warrant for the capture of Samuel Salman El Reda, a Colombian citizen thought to be living in Lebanon, alleged to have coordinated a Hezbollah cell that carried out the bombing; he was subsequently added to the INTERPOL Red Notice list.

The Argentine government shifted its stance in 2011 with respect to engagement with Iran over the AMIA bombing issue. President Fernández indicated Argentina's willingness to enter into a dialogue with the Iranian government despite its refusal to turn over suspects in the case. Several rounds of talks with Iran were held in 2012, with Argentine Foreign Minister Hector Timerman leading the effort.

In January 2013, Argentina announced that it had reached an agreement with Iran, and signed a memorandum of understanding to establish a joint Truth Commission made up of impartial jurists from third countries to review the bombing case. After extensive debate, Argentina's Congress completed its approval of the agreement on February 28, 2013. Argentina's two main Jewish groups, AMIA and the Delegation of Israeli Associations (DAIA), strongly opposed the agreement because they believe that it could guarantee impunity for the Iranian suspects.[49] Several U.S. Members of Congress also expressed their strong concerns about the Truth Commission because they believed it could jeopardize Argentina's AMIA investigation and charges against the Iranians.

In May 2014, an Argentine court declared unconstitutional the agreement with Iran to jointly investigate the AMIA bombing. Special Prosecutor Nisman had maintained that the agreement with Iran constituted an "undue interference of the executive branch in the exclusive sphere of the judiciary."[50] The Fernández government maintained that it would appeal the ruling to Argentina's Supreme Court.

In a speech before the United Nations General Assembly on September 24, 2014, President Fernández acknowledged the 20th anniversary of the AMIA bombing, and expressed support for the memorandum of understanding with Iran, maintaining that it would enable the accused Iranian citizens to make statements before an Argentine judge. Fernández also said that Jewish organizations in Argentina accused the government of complicity with the state of Iran because of the agreement on the AMIA investigation.[51] DAIA President Julio Schlosser criticized the President's U.N. speech, maintaining that it was trying to convert the victims into victimizers.[52]

OUTLOOK

Argentina's presidential election is not scheduled until October 2015, but the race is already underway with several contenders, including two from the Peronist party, leading opinion polls to succeed President Fernández, who will be completing her second term in office. At this juncture, Argentina is facing a difficult economic situation, with the IMF forecasting economic contraction in 2014 and 2015. While the government has taken significant actions over the past year to repair its international economic relations (including resolving investment disputes and reaching a deal with Paris Club creditors), its outstanding dispute with holdout creditors is impeding the country's access to international credit markets. Some observers speculate that the government will make efforts to resolve the dispute in 2015, once a clause requiring creditors to be treated equally expires. Such a move, however, could also prove difficult for the Fernández government since it has led a public campaign strongly criticizing the holdout creditors. Many observers believe that any of the leading candidates for president would espouse more market-friendly policies than the current government.

U.S.-Argentine relations generally are characterized by robust commercial relations and cooperation in a number of areas, including nonproliferation, human rights, education, and science and technology. There have, however, been tensions at various times in the bilateral relationship, including the current U.S. judicial case regarding the holdouts, and Argentine officials at times have lashed out at the United States. Resolution of the issue would likely lead to improvement in the tenor of relations. Moreover, Argentina's 2015 presidential elections will also likely bring to power a government more committed to maintaining constructive bilateral relations.

APPENDIX. SELECTED U.S. EXECUTIVE BRANCH REPORTS

Bilateral Relations Fact Sheet, U.S. Relations with Argentina, State Department, November 21, 2013.http://www.state.gov/r/pa/ei/ bgn/ 26516.htm

Congressional Budget Justification for Foreign Operations FY2015, Annex 3: Regional Perspectives (p. 637), State Department, April 18, 2014. http://www.state.gov/documents/organization/224070.pdf

Country Reports on Human Rights Practices 2013, Argentina, State Department, February 27, 2014. http://www.state.gov/j/drl/rls/hrrpt/ humanrig htsreport/index.htm?year=2013&dlid=220414

Country Reports on Terrorism 2013 (Western Hemisphere Overview), State Department, April 2014. http://www.state.gov/j/ct/rls/crt/2013/ 224825. htm

Doing Business in Argentina, U.S. Department of Commerce, 2014. http://www.export.gov/argentina/doingbusinessinargentina/index.asp

International Religious Freedom Report 2013, Argentina, State Department, July 28, 2014. http://www.state.gov/j/drl/rls/irf/religiousfreedom/ index. htm?year=2013&dlid=222351

International Narcotics Control Strategy Report 2014, Vol. I, Argentina, State Department, March 2014. http://www.state.gov/j/inl/rls/nrcrpt/2014/ vol1/222841.htm

International Narcotics Control Strategy Report 2014, Vol. II, Argentina, State Department, March 2014. http://www.state.gov/j/inl/rls/nrcrpt/2014/vol2/222681.htm

Investment Climate Statement, 2014, Argentina, State Department, June 2014. http://www.state.gov/e/eb/rls/othr/ics/2014/226872.htm

National Trade Estimate Report on Foreign Trade Barriers, 2014, Argentina, Office of the United States Trade Representative, March 31, 2014. http://www.ustr.gov/sites/default/files/2014%20NTE%20Report%20on%20FTB%20Argentina.pdf

End Notes

[1] Peronism as a political movement dates to the 1940s when Juan Domingo Peron, a colonel serving as Secretary of Labor in a military government that assumed power in 1943, went on to build a formidable political base through support from the rapidly growing union movement. Peron was ousted by the military in 1955, but after 18 years of exile, he returned and was reelected president in 1973. He died a year later and was succeeded by his second wife Isabel, who had little political experience. Economic and political chaos ensued, with political violence surging and the country experiencing its first bout of hyperinflation. The military intervened in 1976, and ruled until the return to democracy in 1983. Today in Argentina, Peronism has many different factions across the political spectrum.

[2] "Modest Victory Fails to Mask Uncertain Future for Kirchnerismo," Latin American Weekly Report, October 31, 2013.

[3] Sources for the section include: "Argentina: Key Figures," Economist Intelligence Unit (EIU) ViewsWire, September 24, 2014; and "Country Report Argentina, EIU, November 2014.

[4] "Argentine Presidential Election 25 October 2013, and Runoff 24 November," MercoPress, September 3, 2014.

[5] "Argentine Agency Looks at President's Approval Rating," BBC Monitoring Americas, text of report from the official Argentine news agency Telam, November 10, 2014.

[6] "Argentina: Small Town Stand for a Big Alliance?" LatinNews Daily, September 8, 2014.

[7] "Argentina Politics: Quick View – Máximo Kirchner Steps into the Spotlight," EIU ViewsWire, September 25, 2014; and "Cristina Candidata?" El Cronista Comercial (Argentina), May 30 2014.

[8] "Argentina: On the Death of Jorge Rafael Videla," Human Rights Watch, May 17, 2013; and Jonathan Gilbert, "Argentine Judge Orders Arrest of Spanish Ex-Officials," New York Times, November 2, 2014.

[9] Human Rights Watch, World Report 2014; and U.S. Department of State, Country Reports on Human Rights Practices 2013, February 2014.

[10] "The Battle for Clarín," LatinNews Daily Report, October 9, 2014; "Argentina, Media War, The Government's Media Regulatory Agency is Forcing a Reorganization of the Clarín Group under the Country's Broadcast Media Law," Reporters Without Borders, October 23, 2014.

[11] Because of doubts about the accuracy of Argentina's economic statistics, the World Bank estimates that the country's per capita income is within the range of an upper middle

income economy, between $4,086 and $12,615. See World Bank, World Development Report 2014, 2013. The International Monetary Fund (IMF) estimates Argentina's gross domestic product per capita as $14,709 in 2013. See IMF, World Economic Outlook Database, October 2014 edition.

[12] U.N. Economic Commission for Latin America and the Caribbean, Social Panorama of Latin America 2013, March 2014.

[13] "Country Report Argentina," EIU, October 2014.

[14] IMF, World Economic Outlook: Legacies, Clouds, Uncertainties, October 2014.

[15] "Country Report Argentina," EIU, November 2014.

[16] "Argentina: Dark Clouds Gathering," LatinNews Daily, September 24, 2014.

[17] World Bank, "New WBG Strategy to Support Poverty Reduction & Inclusive Growth in Argentina," Press Release, September 9, 2014.

[18] "Country Report Argentina," EIU, November 2014.

[19] The Paris Club is an informal group of 19 creditor nations, including the United States, Canada, Japan, and many European countries. The group meets about 10 times annually to collaborate on official debt workout mechanisms for developing countries. "Paris Club Confirms First Receipt of Argentine Arrears," Reuters News, August 4, 2014.

[20] "Country Report Argentina," EIU, September 20014.

[21] U.S. Department of State, "U.S. Relations with Argentina," Fact Sheet, November 21, 2013.

[22] U.S. Department of State, "Update on Seizure of U.S. Cargo by Argentine Authorities," Fact Sheet, February 17, 2011.

[23] Ken Parks and Julian E. Barnes, "World News: U.S., Argentina in Tussle Over Seized Cargo," Wall Street Journal, February 16, 2011.

[24] U.S. trade statistics are from the Department of Commerce, as presented by Global Trade Atlas. Argentina's trade partners were derived from Argentine statistics presented by Global Trade Atlas.

[25] Brian Flood, "WTO Dispute Panel Rules Against Argentina in Challenge to Import Licensing Restrictions," International Trade Reporter, August 22, 2014.

[26] U.S. Department of Commerce, "U.S. Direct Investment Abroad Tables," Survey of Current Business, September 2014.

[27] U.S. Department of State, 2014 Investment Climate Statement – Argentina, June 2014. In March 2012, the United States suspended Argentina's eligibility as a beneficiary of the Generalized System of Preferences (GSP), a preferential tariff treatment program, because of Argentina's failure to enforce such arbitral awards. About 11% of U.S. imports from Argentina benefitted from GSP in 2011. The GSP program, however, expired at the end of July 2013, and Congress has not renewed it. For more on GSP, see CRS Report RL33663, Generalized System of Preferences: Background and Renewal Debate, by Vivian C. Jones, and CRS Report RS22541, Generalized System of Preferences: Agricultural Imports, by Renée Johnson.

[28] U.S. Department of State, 2014 Investment Climate Statement – Argentina, June 2014; Martin Hutchinson, "Playing Nice Starts to Pay Off for Argentina," Reuters News, May 29, 2014.

[29] Office of the United States Trade Representative, 2014 Special 301 Report, April 2014.

[30] U.S. Department of State, Assistant Secretary of State, Bureau of Western Hemisphere Affairs, Roberta S. Jacobson, "U.S. Priorities in the Western Hemisphere," September 26, 2014.

[31] Taos Turner, "Argentina Warns U.S. Diplomat Over Remarks to Local Newspaper," Dow Jones Newswires, September 16, 2014.

[32] "Presidenta: 'Si Me Pas Algo, Que Nadie Mire Hacia el Oriente, Miren Hacia el Norte,'" Agencia Diarios y Noticias (Buenos Aires), September 30, 2014; Cristina Fernández Says 'Look North' If Anything Happens to Her," Telesur, October 1, 2014.

[33] Some of the material in this section is drawn from CRS Report R41029, Argentina's Defaulted Sovereign Debt: Dealing with the "Holdouts," by J. F. Hornbeck.

[34] See CRS Report R41029, Argentina's Defaulted Sovereign Debt: Dealing with the "Holdouts", by J. F. Hornbeck

[35] For more on the Paris Club, see CRS Report RS21482, The Paris Club and International Debt Relief, by Martin A. Weiss.

[36] Ken Parks, "Argentina to Start Debt Talks with Paris Club on Wednesday," Wall Street Journal, May 27, 2014.

[37] Paris Club Press Release, May 29, 2014, http://www.clubdeparis.org/sections/communication/communiques/ argentine/viewLanguage/en.

[38] Leigh Thomas, "Paris Club Invites Argentina to Hold Debt Negotiation," Reuters, March 14, 2014

[39] Leigh Thomas and Sarah Marsh, "Argentina Clinches Landmark Debt Repayment Deal with Paris Club," Reuters, May 29, 2014.

[40] Richard Deitz, "A Sensible Path for Avoiding an Argentine Default," Wall Street Journal, July 2, 2014; Alison Frankel, "The Other Loser in Argentina Debt Saga: U.S. Courts," Reuters, July 31, 2014.

[41] Bob Van Voris, "Argentina Faces $4.7 Billion in New Bond Suits, Bloomberg News, November 7, 2014.

[42] Richard Deitz, "A Sensible Path for Avoiding an Argentine Default," Wall Street Journal, July 2, 2014.

[43] Thomas Landon, Jr., "Argentine Economist Says Bond Holdouts Should be Paid," New York Times, September 3, 2014.

[44] Fabiana Frayssinet, "Did Argentina Default or Not? It's more than Semantics," Inter Press Service News Agency, August 4, 2014.

[45] Charlie Devereux and Pablo Gonzalez, "Argentina Says Willing to Negotiate with Holdouts Next Year," Bloomberg News, September 26, 2014.

[46] "Argentina: Bond Swap Law Approved," LatinNews Daily, September 12, 2014.

[47] Alexandra Stevenson, "Judge Holds Argentina in Contempt of Court," New York Times, September 30, 2014.

[48] INTERPOL, Media Release, "INTERPOL General Assembly Upholds Executive Committee Decision on AMIA Red Notice Dispute," November 7, 2007. The three other Iranians wanted by Argentina not included on INTERPOL's red notice list are former President Ali Akbar Hashemi-Rafsanjani, former Foreign Minister Ali Akbar Velayati, and former Iranian Ambassador to Argentina Hadi Soleimanpour.

[49] "A Perverse Manoeuvre in Argentina," LatinNews Daily, February 28, 2013.

[50] "Argentine Court Declares Bombing Probe with Iran Unconstitutional," Agence France Presse, May 16, 2014.

[51] "Speech of Argentinian President Cristina Fernández During the UN General Assembly,"

[51] Morocco World News, Video with transcript, available at http://www.moroccoworldnews.com/2014/09/140311/speech-of-argentinianpresident-cristina-fernandez-during-the-un-general-assembly/

[52] "La DAIA Criticó el Discurso de la Presidenta en la ONU," El Cronista (Argentina), September 29, 2014.

In: Argentina
Editor: Eileen Mckinney

ISBN: 978-1-63482-251-0

Chapter 2

ARGENTINA'S POST-CRISIS ECONOMIC REFORM: CHALLENGES FOR U.S. POLICY*

J. F. Hornbeck

SUMMARY

U.S.-Argentine economic relations have long history of mutually beneficial engagement. In recent years, however, they have been strained at times, in part because of Argentina's struggle to maintain macroeconomic stability, and also because of specific policy choices that have made the business environment difficult to navigate since the country's 2001 financial crisis. Following a steep currency devaluation and the largest sovereign default in history, Argentina entered a deep recession with high unemployment and social upheaval. It brought to power a new government, and with it a shift in economic policy away from market-oriented policies toward greater government control of the economy in pursuit of "social equity." The initial policy responses intended to restore order and address the most pressing social problems evolved into permanent social programs. Government policies introduced many distortions into the economy, including high inflation, which have required regular adjustments in the international accounts to maintain economic stability. These include managed trade, capital controls, and

* This is an edited, reformatted and augmented version of a Congressional Research Service publication R43022, prepared for Members and Committees of Congress, dated April 15, 2013.

limited currency conversion, among other policies that have earned the ire of international stakeholders.

Argentina's economic policies reflect priority for financial independence, social equity, and what may be considered a commitment to "populist" macroeconomic solutions. Even in recognizing that countries can govern themselves well under alternative policy frameworks, what stands out for many is the sense that Argentina's policy choices, with attendant economic distortions, increase the risk of a new financial crisis. The resulting spillovers into international economic policy are unavoidable. Trade protection, managed exchange rates, and capital controls, for example, are policy adjustments required to address problems that materialize in a constrained economic system (e.g., subsidy-driven fiscal expansion, price controls, inability to borrow internationally) that cannot easily accommodate current account deficits, a market exchange rate, or standard macroeconomic responses to high inflation.

Congress and private U.S. stakeholders have opposed many of Argentina's policies that include a sovereign default on debt owed to both private investors and countries, including the United States; refusal to pay awards ordered by the International Centre for the Settlement of Investment Disputes (ICSID); nationalization of foreign assets; trade protectionism; capital and currency controls; and refusal to abide by International Monetary Fund (IMF) reporting requirements. Some U.S. investors are suing the government of Argentina in U.S. federal courts; the Obama Administration has invoked financial restrictions, revoked trade preferences, voted against loans for Argentina in the development banks, and filed cases before the World Trade Organization (WTO). Some Members of Congress have expressed dissatisfaction in hearings, resolutions, and proposed legislation.

International stakeholders, both public and private, find themselves challenged by this system, along with some Argentines. One indication of the breadth of international dissatisfaction over Argentina's policies is the call for effectively removing Argentina from the G-20, despite the lack of precedent and formal procedure for doing so. Irrespective of these initiatives, Argentina has not been moved to change course, and Congress may decide to consider once again U.S. options for addressing bilateral concerns with Argentina.

At the close of 2001, Argentina plunged into a devastating financial crisis. Deep recession, high unemployment, and social upheaval brought to power a new government, and with it a new direction in economic policy away from market-oriented policies toward greater government control of the economy. A new emphasis on "social equity" placed additional strain on the budget, but economic recovery, strong foreign demand for Argentine commodities, an expansive monetary policy, and debt repudiation brought six straight years of fiscal surplus. By 2012, however, the creeping deterioration of Argentina's economic fortunes was undeniable. Slowing economic growth, rising inflation, and a tightening budget constraint raised doubts about the country's fiscal capacity to meet the now well-entrenched "populist" expectations. At risk is the Argentine economic model itself, as well as the political and social balance it has supported over the past decade.

Supporting an expansive domestic policy agenda has led to a highly distorted economy that in turn has required repeated intervention in the external accounts to maintain a fragile balance. Debt repudiation, expropriation, capital and currency controls, trade protectionism, and refusal to abide by judgments made by international organizations are part of the policy mix that has also created tension with foreign governments, international financial institutions, and private sector interests. In the United States, the federal courts and the Obama Administration have taken action against many of Argentina's foreign economic policies. Previous Congresses have introduced legislation and resolutions denouncing Argentina's practices, and Congress may consider whether to formally respond to Argentina's foreign economic policy as well. This report provides a framework for understanding Argentina's economic policies, issues raised for U.S. stakeholders, and implications for the future of U.S.-Argentine economic relations.

U.S. Economic Interests and the Post-Crisis Political Economy

U.S.-Argentine economic relations have long history of mutually beneficial engagement. Still, Argentina is only the United States' 29th-largest export market and 54th in imports, and accounts for less than 0.05% of total U.S. trade. The United States is Argentina's fourth-largest export market and number three in imports, accounting for roughly 8% of Argentine trade, but falling well behind Brazil and China. U.S. foreign direct investment (FDI) in Argentina is third-highest in South America behind Brazil and Chile, and reflects the many U.S. firms operating for decades in all sectors of the Argentine economy.

Nonetheless, U.S.-Argentina economic relations have been strained at times, in part because of Argentina's struggle to maintain macroeconomic stability, and also because of specific policy choices that have made the business environment difficult to navigate. For these reasons, elaborated in this report, bilateral trade has remained small and U.S. investment has stalled over the past decade. For example, from 1993 to 2000, when Argentina had stabilized its economy from the hyperinflation of the late 1980s, the U.S. investment position rose by nearly 300%, from $4.4 billion to $17.5 billion. In response to the 2001 financial crisis and subsequent policy changes, FDI fell precipitously to $9.2 billion in 2004. Although it has since recovered, FDI stood at $13.3 billion in 2011, a 25% decline from 2000 levels.[1] These trends reflect many problems that have developed for U.S. stakeholders over the economic policies Argentina has adopted since 2001. The problems have become increasingly difficult in recent years because of deteriorating economic conditions that have led the Argentine government to tighten controls over many facets of the economy.

To a great extent, Argentina's approach to domestic governance and international economic relations, including the friction it has caused with the United States and other stakeholders, can be understood in the context of its response to the financial turmoil that followed in the aftermath of the 2001-2002 economic collapse. The fixed exchange rate convertibility program that had anchored the economy since 1991 became untenable, as did the government of President Fernando de la Rua. In 2001, after three years of nagging recession, economic output collapsed into a two-year free fall (see *Table 1*). Argentina found itself deeply in debt, which forced it to adopt severe austerity measures even as much of the income and wealth of its citizens disappeared virtually overnight. Poverty and unemployment skyrocketed, riots broke out, and violence filled the streets. Intervening presidents (five in twice as many days) oversaw a steep currency devaluation, the largest sovereign default in history,[2] and highly restrictive management of the financial sector.

Social upheaval led to political uncertainty and ultimately a succession of presidents who shared a vision of major economic policy reform. The Argentine Congress took the first step toward reestablishing political stability by appointing to the presidency Senator Eduardo Duhalde, a long-time leader of the Peronist party (Partido Justicialista—PJ). He assumed office on January 1, 2002, to complete de la Rua's unexpired term. In the national elections that followed in 2003, Argentines elected another Peronist, Néstor Kirchner, who was succeeded by his wife, Cristina Fernández de Kirchner, in the 2007 and 2011 elections. Each administration took a closer step toward institutionalizing what is frequently referred to as a "populist" economic program that has come to define Argentine political and economic reality in the 21st century.[3]

President Duhalde made clear from the outset that he blamed Argentina's economic crisis on a failure of the free market system, and he vowed to change course. Under emergency economic powers ceded to him by Congress, he eliminated the currency board that had anchored economic policy, devalued the peso, limited bank and foreign currency transactions, and oversaw the passage of bankruptcy laws that restricted payments to foreign nationals. At the same time, social policy became the new priority. He initiated subsidies for transportation and energy that in time became fully entrenched in the federal budget. Given the lack of revenue options, new temporary taxes were put on exports and financial transactions. In time these grew and became permanent, with proceeds dedicated to social spending.

Under Presidents Kirchner and Fernández, these initial policy responses intended to restore order and address the most pressing social problems became permanent programs. As the recovery took hold, Argentina could afford some fiscal largesse because of favorable terms of trade and the strong global demand for Argentine commodities, which contributed to nine years of strong economic growth (see *Table 1*).[4]

Table 1. Argentina: Selected Economic Data, 2000-2012

	2000	*2001*	*2002*	*2003*	*2004*	*2005*	*2006*	*2007*	*2008*	*2009*	*2010*	*2011*	*2012*
GDP Growth (%)	-0.8	-4.4	-10.9	8.8	9.0	9.2	8.5	8.7	6.8	0.9	9.2	8.9	2.2
Overall Fiscal Balance (% of GDP)	-3.6	-6.8	-2.0	0.9	3.7	2.1	1.9	0.6	0.7	-0.8	-0.1	-2.3	-1.6
Primary Fiscal Balance	0.4	-1.3	0.7	2.8	5.3	4.4	4.0	2.7	2.8	1.4	1.5	-0.1	0.5
(% of GDP)													
Public Debt (% GDP)	45.7	53.7	166.3	138.2	126.4	72.8	63.6	55.7	48.5	48.5	45.1	41.2	39.9
Inflation Rate INDEC	-0.7	-1.5	41.0	3.7	6.1	12.3	9.8	8.5	7.2	7.7	10.9	9.5	10.2
(%)a													
Inflation Rate (adjusted)									25.0	18.1	22.4	25.1	25.4
(%)[a]													
Real Avg. Wages (index)			76.0	85.2	93.1	100.0	108.9	118.8	129.2	144.3	163.0	196.1	231.8
Current Acct Balance (% GDP)	-3.1	-1.4	8.5	6.3	2.1	2.9	3.6	2.8	1.5	2.1	0.8	-0.3	0.2

Table 1. (Continued)

	2000	*2001*	*2002*	*2003*	*2004*	*2005*	*2006*	*2007*	*2008*	*2009*	*2010*	*2011*	*2012*
Terms of Trade (index)				91.0	95.3	100.0	106.8	109.6	113.0	103.3	113.4	120.3	119.6
Real Effective Exchange Rate Index[b]			106.9	97.5	100.2	100.0	102.0	101.2	97.2	99.3	98.5	96.0	93.6
International Reserves	32.5	15.3	10.4	13.8	19.3	27.3	31.2	45.7	46.2	48.0	52.2	46.4	45.3
($ bn)													
International Bond Issues ($ mn)[c]	13,468	2,711	0	100	200	540	1,896	3,256	65	500	3,146	2,193	663

Source: United Nations Economic Commission on Latin America and the Caribbean (ECLAC), Preliminary Overview of the Economies of Latin America and the Caribbean, December 2012. Indexes with 2005 base year do not include data prior to 2003.

[a] Instituto Nacional de Estadística y Censos (INDEC)—Argentina's official government statistical office, which has come under criticism for understating inflation rates since 2007. The line below presents adjusted annual inflation rates since 2008 that reflect the simple average of inflation rates reported at the beginning of each month as computed by an academic team at MIT. They match closely many other estimates offered by private consultants. See http://www.InfacionVerdadera.com and Alberto Cavallo, "Online and Official Price Indexes: Measuring Argentina's Inflation," *Journal of Monetary Economics*, vol. 60, no. 1.

[b] A decrease in the index reflects a real appreciation of the peso exchange rate.

[c] Includes sovereign, financial sector, and other commercial debt.

Expansive fiscal and monetary policies reinforced growth and debt repudiation freed up fiscal resources in the name of national economic independence. The government disdained reliance on foreign financing and what it considered the meddling of international institutions and foreign governments, many of which were held to be complicit in the economic catastrophe that befell the country a decade earlier. As a result, Argentina's foreign economic policies were largely subordinated to the domestic political agenda, with limited concern for their impact on foreign interests.

THE NEW MACROECONOMIC FRAMEWORK

The new economic policy framework came with many tradeoffs including an increasingly large fiscal burden, rising inflation, and, as discussed below, questionable ad hoc policy adjustments imposed to counter the effects of economic distortions as they arose. A near-term economic crisis in Argentina may not be at hand, but protests over rising costs are becoming more frequent and surveys conducted by the Universidad Torcuato Di Tella point to sharply declining confidence in the government beginning in 2012.[5] Many economists suggest that it may be too late to engineer a soft landing, raising serious questions about the sustainability of the current economic model, and perhaps stability of the political system as well.

Fiscal Challenges and Constraints

From 2003 through 2011, Argentina's economy grew robustly with the exception of the 2008 global downturn. From 2003 through 2008, the government ran a fiscal surplus, reflective of strong growth in public revenue. At the same time, public debt as a percent of GDP also declined steadily, which on the surface suggests that the Argentine economy had not been performing badly. Nonetheless, there has been a continuing erosion of the fiscal position since 2003, as may be seen in *Table 1*, with the balance turning to deficit in 2009 and thereafter. Also, the public debt ratio stabilized more or less by 2010, and economic growth declined noticeably in 2012, with no expectation of returning to previous high levels. These trends reflect a near-term deterioration in the internal economic situation, in part related to policy distortions, beginning with the fiscal accounts.

The Argentine government directly intervenes in the operation of the economy to achieve, in its own words, "economic development with social equity."[6] This focus is not new to Argentina and requires extensive fiscal effort. On the spending side, public policy pursues equity through social transfers: setting the price and domestic supply of key consumer goods (e.g., energy and food); providing direct subsidies for energy and transportation; and adjusting salaries to offset inflation. Subsidies began under President Duhalde, in part to meet the basic needs of those thrust into poverty. The cost and array of programs, however, have expanded, contributing to rising fiscal deficits since 2006. Subsidies grew from US$1.6 billion in 2005 to US$18.1 billion in 2011, equaling 4% of GDP. They are distributed among energy (56% of total), public transportation (30%), and other public services (14%).[7]

For years, the Argentine government has periodically capped prices and restricted exports of certain key food products, including at times staples such as beef. On February 4, 2013, it took the added step of negotiating a price freeze on food and other household goods with the major supermarket chains. The Fernández government is also reportedly considering extending the freeze until the fall 2013 election.[8] These practices reduce costs to consumers, with the intention of stimulating consumption and improving income distribution, but have also distorted market signals for wholesalers and producers. The agricultural sector has borne a large part of this cost, resulting in protests and interruptions in production, reducing profits and taxes paid by food producers.

Energy is the largest of the public subsidies, amounting to over 2% of GDP.[9] Given that energy production has actually fallen in Argentina, largely due to price controls that have dampened investment, the government has had to make up the difference through imports. In effect, oil and natural gas, the predominant forms of energy use, are imported at international prices, and then deeply discounted and distributed to the population. This policy compromises both the fiscal and current account balances by raising costs to the government and increasing demand for imports.

Finally, many private and public sector salaries, including those for union members and pensioners, have been adjusted annually to the increase in the price level (25% in 2012; see below) to ensure that rising inflation does not erode purchasing power for key constituents. It is perhaps no coincidence that real wages (adjusted for inflation) grew by 5% or more immediately preceding the presidential elections of 2007 and 2011, while declining afterward.[10] In addition, the number of public employees and those relying on public retirement and social programs has risen from 5.3 million individuals in 2001 (14.4% of total population) to 13.2 million in 2011 (32.2% of total population), adding substantially to the fiscal burden.[11]

Given that the current government has been strongly supported by groups that benefit disproportionally from subsidies, price controls, wage adjustments, and public employment, there is a political rationale for sustaining them, but they come with significant costs and tradeoffs. On the revenue side, Argentina has benefitted from sustained global demand for its export commodities, a major source of tax revenue.[12] The federal government has also relied on monetary expansion, foreign debt repudiation, heavy income taxation, and increased intragovernmental borrowing. These options, however, may be reaching their limits. Argentina's fiscal deficits would be addressed by most countries with a combination of financing options. The government, however, faces a number of constraints that make this difficult.

To meet its budgetary goals, Argentina must work within three options. It may raise taxes, issue debt, or print money to cover government expenditures. First, income taxation is already heavily skewed toward the upper-middle income groups. The national income tax rate is 38%, but by one estimate, only half the working population actually pays taxes, so the effective rate on average can be twice that, which constrains further tax increases.[13] This is one reason the government has turned increasingly to alternative sources of revenue, such as taxes on financial transactions, and particularly exports, which rose from 11.8% to 20.5% of tax revenue from 2006 to 2011.[14]

Second, since defaulting on its sovereign debt in 2002, the federal government has had no access to international bond markets, nor has it signaled any desire to return to this option. If the government is to increase borrowing, it must continue to do so internally. Third, although Argentina has expanded the money supply to cover shortfalls (see next section), this too may be limited at some point by inflation and the price and social instability it can produce.

Given the constraints it faces, and that tax revenue fell from 19.0% to 11.4% of GDP from 2006 to 2011, the Argentine government has chosen a policy mix designed to self-finance public expenditures, relying largely on the resources of government agencies and monetary expansion. Pension funds have provided one source of cash. In 2007, the Kirchner government nationalized private pension funds, dedicating their revenue streams, and those of the National Social Security Administration (ANSeS-FGS), to the purchase of government bonds at interest rates set by the Treasury, typically well below the actual inflation rate. The government also relies on loans from the government-owned Banco de la Nación Argentina[15] and "temporary overdrafts" from the Central Bank to meet financing gaps. In 2012, it met most of its financing needs from these sources. This trend is expected to continue, and perhaps be extended to other social and health service institutions (e.g., *Obras Sociales*—Social Works) to finance government operations.[16]

Financing government spending in this manner has certain benefits. The government does not have to rely on external sources and is assured that maturing debt can be rolled over on a predictable basis and at an accommodating interest rate. Should the government find itself unable to meet payments, being a creditor to itself allows flexibility for working out financial shortfalls.

On the other hand, Argentina's financing arrangements also raise many questions regarding longterm sustainability. Although the government points to reduced debt ratios (see *Table 1*), it uses intra-government transfers to place significant amounts of debt in public agencies.[17] Should a fiscal crisis occur, Argentina defaults on itself, potentially forcing the retirement system into insolvency.[18] A tax structure based on exports and financial transactions raises costs, particularly to export, and so can diminish incentives to produce and invest, which ultimately may reduce revenue, as well as economic growth. In fact, industrial production fell by 3.8% in 2012 for the first time in more than 10 years.[19] Argentine goods are also less competitive in global markets, suggesting that these financing schemes risk jeopardizing long-term growth and development.

Monetary Policy: Accommodation?

The main feature of Argentina's monetary policy is its expansionist orientation, which supports growth, fiscal, and exchange rate targets. Despite the Central Bank's (*Banco Central de la República*—BCRA's) claims of policy neutrality or what it refers to as "autarky,"[20] the preponderance of evidence, discussed below, points to an institution whose primary mission is to accommodate the national government's overall economic policy agenda. This shift has occurred incrementally, a key milestone occurring in 2010, when the then-president of the BCRA refused to use its resources to finance government spending, a showdown that resulted in his forced resignation.

The transition continued with the new Central Bank Charter, which entered into force on April 6, 2012. The charter formally restates the mission of the BCRA, eliminating price stability as a key policy goal and replacing it with a new mandate to "promote monetary stability, financial stability, employment, and economic development with social equity."[21] In addition, the charter emphasizes the BCRA's role in credit allocation, particularly for longer-term productive investments. The required ratio of the international reserves to the monetary base was also eliminated, providing flexibility to manage and use BCRA reserves as needed and determined by the Board of Directors. Monetary policy operates through multiple channels, using both money creation and BCRA reserves to support key government goals of maintaining positive fiscal and current account balances, a stable exchange rate, and credit expansion.

Money Creation

The new bank charter defines the central goal of the BCRA as maintaining "monetary stability," which is a vague concept by conventional standards, but is generally interpreted to mean maintaining a stable exchange rate rather than price stability, the more common goal of central banks. Meeting fiscal, current account, and growth targets are also in the mix. Monetary expansion is at the heart of this strategy, and currently, Argentina has one of the most expansive monetary policies in Latin America.[22]

The goal of an expansive monetary policy is to finance the deficit, purchase dollars for the international reserve position, and have the liquidity to manage volatility of the peso exchange rate. The money supply, however, is also the main cause of inflation, which should lead to a depreciating peso if Argentina is to remain competitive globally. The government actively manages the exchange rate. It allows for a steady nominal depreciation, but because it is not sufficient to adjust fully for inflation, the currency is actually experiencing a real appreciation. A higher-valued peso makes exporting, already burdened by taxes, relatively more difficult, thereby requiring restrictions on imports at times to maintain a balanced current account.

In recent years, Argentina has relied on the dollar inflows from a current account surplus to balance dollar outflows from the financial account to cover foreign payments.[23] Should the current account also turn to deficit, the alternative is to use international reserves. Reserves levels, however, have already fallen by over 22% since 2010 and stood at $40.5 billion as of March 27, 2013.[24] In addition, there are increasing reports of declines in dollar deposits in the banking system spurred in part over fears that the government will exchange them for pesos if it needs to, as it did in 2002.[25]

Among the key monetary objectives is to increase the amount of dollars held in reserve and the amount of pesos circulating in the domestic economy. The BCRA fine tunes this process at times by "sterilizing" the monetary growth effect of dollar purchases. That is, if policymakers determine that dollar purchases must continue, causing the monetary base to expand too fast, they can counteract the monetary growth by having the BCRA purchase pesos through the sales of financial instruments such as repurchase agreements and bonds. For example, in 2012, foreign exchange purchases accounted for 85% of the monetary expansion, but were offset in part by short-term sales of these financial instruments.[26]

Management of the foreign exchange market, as complex and finely tuned as the process is in Argentina, has not fully offset the monetary effects of dollar inflows, reinforcing rapid growth in monetary aggregates. In 2012, M2 expanded by 29% and M3 by 32%.[27] In this way, the Fernández government created financial resources that could be used to cover budget shortfalls. Argentina is effectively "monetizing" public debt on one hand, and managing its external accounts on the other to support spending. The cost is inflation, which should rise with the increase in money supply. The inflationary spiral completes the circle, reinforced by an expansive fiscal policy needed for subsidies, income support, price caps, and other social transfers. Consumers are also enticed to spend rather than save given rising prices. Inflation expectations, therefore, are built into a "vicious cycle," the sustainability of which is becoming questionable. Inflation also encourages flight to dollars, making them increasingly valuable as a store of value. In response, Argentina instituted foreign exchange controls and limited currency conversion.

Inflation Accounting

Inflation has become a structural element of the Argentine economy and foundational to executing the government's overall economic policy. An issue that has become difficult for Argentina's government is the allegation of official underreporting or outright manipulation of inflation data since 2007. Estimates by many independent economists and other indicators of changes in the price level challenge government reporting. The *Economist*, in an unusual move, has dropped official reporting of inflation data in favor of independent unofficial estimates. A deepening concern has been the pressure exerted by the Fernández government to mute independent economist estimates in Argentina with fines and threats of imprisonment.[28]

Inflation reported by the *Instituto Nacional de Estadística y Censos* (INDEC), Argentina's official statistical agency, has been challenged since 2007, when the Kirchner government decided to replace the director with a political appointee. Since then, in most years, the discrepancy between Argentina's officially reported inflation rate and other estimates of inflation has grown. In 2012, INDEC reported that inflation rose by approximately 10% annually. Private-sector and provincial government estimates place it above 25%. Government reporting on nominal wage increases reinforces these estimates given that public- and private-sector wages have been adjusted upward by over 25% for both 2011 and 2012, rates presumably in line with maintaining purchasing power.[29]

An academic team at the Massachusetts Institute of Technology (MIT) has weighed in with more robust statistical analysis by comparing INDEC inflation reporting with indexes they produced from daily online price data. Whereas these data were able "to match both the average level of annual inflation and the long-run inflation trends" for four Latin American countries that produce accurate inflation statistics, they uncovered the large and growing discrepancy in Argentina between INDEC and other price level indicators. They conclude that the online data estimates "tend to be two to three times higher than official inflation," yet dynamic trends, or the movement of inflation upward and downward, are consistent.[30]

The Argentine government argues that it is difficult to measure inflation precisely, and that a moderate amount of inflation is broadly accepted as a structural element of the economy as part of the tradeoff for meeting economic growth and social equity goals. The government, however, benefits from underreporting inflation in at least four ways. First, it can postpone policy responses aimed at reducing inflation that are typically austere, highly unpopular, and potentially politically difficult. Second, heavy financial regulation means that the government can dictate its financing terms (interest rates, maturity terms) on domestic debt. Third, domestic debt can be inflated away and, fourth, some 25% of Argentina's public debt is indexed to inflation, as are many social spending programs. By underreporting inflation, costs of program spending and borrowing have been lower than they otherwise would have been. To date, estimates of government saving from underreporting inflation are as high as $2 billion.[31]

There are also costs to the bias in inflation reporting. It affects income bracket measures for purposes of taxation and poverty determinations, effectively understating both, and calls into question the credibility of real GDP calculations.[32] In addition, for all practical purposes, there is no easy correction to the inflation reporting system given that much of economic policy rests on the assumption of lower official inflation estimates. The alternative would be to recognize the real inflation rate, which would likely require a policy correction through monetary contraction, a likely politically disastrous option.

Credit Rationing

The BCRA has taken an active role in using its regulatory power and banking reserves to extend credit to the Argentine economy. In 2007, the Fernández government required the BCRA to create the Bicentennial Productive Financing Program. The BCRA auctions bonds, lending the proceeds for medium- and long-term capital investment, at fixed, and effectively, subsidized interest rates. To date it has allocated US$4.4 billion and disbursed US$2.4 billion.[33] A 2009 law created the Bicentennial Fund for Stability and Debt Reduction and a follow-on decree established the Argentine

Debt Reduction Fund to assure creditors that finances would be available for scheduled payments by setting aside international dollar reserves. For 2013, Argentina has set aside $8.0 billion of international reserves to guarantee international payments.[34]

The BCRA also relies on temporary overdrafts of international reserves to provide short-term financing to the treasury. In addition, the central bank charter reform permits the use of "free available international reserves" to "subscribe" to the Argentine debt relief fund. These funds are used to retire public debt held by the private sector, international financial institutions, and other official bilateral entities.[35] In 2012, the BCRA also created a credit line for private sector "productive investment" in which the largest "financial entities," public and private, are required to finance capital goods and other long-term investment projects. The new program provides medium-term private sector loans for projects that the market is otherwise unwilling to do. A minimum of 50% of loans under this program must be made to micro-, small-, and medium-sized firms. The BCRA justifies this approach as part of its mandate to take on the tasks relegated to development banks in other countries.[36]

Ultimately, these various programs stretch central bank resources in highly unusual ways and distort credit allocation relative to market signals, which no longer fully function in the financial sector. In effect, the government acts to ration credit, financing voids that it has created in a highly regulated economy with a high inflation rate that discourages saving and long-term investment. In 2012, most credit was short term and offered at interest rates of 30%-35% for consumer and credit card loans. Despite the high cost, from 2003 to 2012, consumer loans have grown from 15% to 40% of total private lending, reflecting an increasing bias toward consumption driven by a policy (and hence expectation) of rising inflation.[37] Other loan rates ranged from mortgages at 14.7% to pledge-backed debt of 22.0%, which amounts to negative real interest rates or subsidized lending given an annual inflation rate of 25%.[38] As such, the government uses the BCRA to execute a policy bias toward targeted credit expansion, which is inherently contradictory to what is generally considered a conventional central bank mission of maintaining price stability.

Finally, in an economy that is experiencing both inflation and interest rate caps, such as on government bonds and bank accounts, the requirement that pension funds and other public and private financial institutions hold assets with "artificially suppressed returns" amounts to what economists refer to as financial repression. Argentina's bonds have interest rates far below the actual inflation rate. Research suggests that historically, a high level of domestic debt has been a major incentive to use inflation to reduce the value of that debt, and combined with financial repression amounts to what some experts refer to as a "de facto default," as the real value of financial assets falls.[39] There are also longer-term costs. Currency and capital controls inhibit investing abroad, requiring locals either to spend or invest at a loss at home. In this situation, there is no incentive to save and every incentive to borrow, leading to lower investment. In fact, BCRA statistics show that whereas consumption has grown to 80% of GDP in 2012, investment has stagnated or declined to 22% of GDP.[40]

International Economic Policy

Given the domestic economic policy goals and constraints outlined above, the challenge for Argentina's international economic policy is to maintain sufficient dollar inflows to preserve adequate reserve levels needed to make future international payments. Exchange rate, trade, and foreign investment policies are all managed to achieve this end. The Fernández government has also prioritized reducing foreign debt to decrease future foreign payments as part of the policy to meet this goal, and setting aside a guaranteed portion of Central Bank reserves to ensure that future payments will be met. It is in this constrained context that Argentine foreign economic policy and reactions by foreign stakeholders can be understood.

Argentina faces a number of constraints in trying to maintain its foreign reserves position. First, as discussed above, it has not been able to borrow internationally since the 2001 default. Second, there are limited portfolio and foreign direct investment inflows to Argentina. Third, borrowing constraints require that Argentina run a current account surplus or small deficit. Exchange rate, trade, and investment policies have all had to be repeatedly fine-tuned to accomplish this goal.

Argentina has benefited from multilateral trade, with the trade account contributing most of the dollar inflows required to meet Argentina's needs. It does maintain, however, relatively high tariffs and numerous nontariff barriers. The government has also resorted to a number of controls to maintain dollar liquidity. Oil export taxes, forced repatriation of foreign currency earnings by insurance and extractive industries, import tariffs, capital controls, and restrictions on the exchange of pesos for dollars have contributed to maintaining foreign exchange reserves. In short, trade policy has leaned protectionist in large part to ensure a current account surplus is maintained and that revenue will be generated to meet fiscal and international reserve goals. While strong exports of commodities may point to a relatively open trade posture, import constraints and export controls argue otherwise.

Managing the exchange rate is even more complicated. To remain competitive globally, inflation would have to be largely offset by depreciating the exchange rate. The Argentine government has allowed the nominal exchange rate to depreciate over time, but the competitiveness problem remains because of the real appreciation discussed above. This trend is evident in the dual exchange rates that have developed. Although the government maintains an official exchange rate against foreign currencies (Brazilian real, U.S. dollar, the Euro), an overvalued peso encourages the creation of informal parallel currency markets. In the case of the U.S. dollar, the so-called Blue Rate is some 50% or more higher than the official rate.[41] To counter the demand for dollars, since November 2011 Argentina has restricted the amount of dollars that can be purchased.

The cost has been a large contraction in the trade surplus in 2012 due largely to the fall in exports, risking reserves levels and increasing the fear of devaluation.[42] While the Argentine government so far has been able to balance domestic and international economic policy priorities, the tradeoff has been heavily controlled international trade policy and financial markets. This result ultimately leads to unwieldy distortions in the overall economy, many of which have played out as contentious economic decisions in the international arena.

POLICY ISSUES

Argentina's macroeconomic framework provides a lens from which to evaluate economic priorities of Argentina's administrations since 2002, and the policy tensions they have created for Argentina and the world. This framework appears to be in part constituent driven, grounded in economic nationalism and redistributive social policy, two themes common to Argentina's political history.[43] The extended pursuit of this strategy, however, runs the risk of it becoming unsustainable as instability creeps into the macroeconomic framework, making it increasingly difficult to manage. High inflation, government price controls, an appreciating currency, a loose monetary program, and the ultimate driver, fiscal deficits, all point in this direction.

Foreign stakeholders have borne much of the cost of these policies, many of them adopted as adjustments necessary to make the domestic agenda and internal accounts balance, at least for the short to medium term. Debt has been repudiated, trade has been constrained, dollar investments are not easily transferred, and other international obligations have been postponed indefinitely or repudiated outright. The major points of contention are discussed below.

Sovereign Default and Private Bondholders[44]

One of Argentina's first acts during the 2001 financial crisis was to default on its sovereign debt. This action brought claims against Argentina from private bondholders, who have sued Argentina in U.S. federal (and other national) courts. Although Argentina's inability to pay in full was, for the most part, accepted, Argentina effectively rejected what at the time were considered standard procedures for organizing a mutually agreed debt resolution. This process typically included developing realistic expectations of macroeconomic adjustments feasible for meeting certain debt repayment terms under the guidance of the International Monetary Fund (IMF). In the past, the "blessing" of the IMF has led to debt restructurings that have avoided costly legal battles. For various reasons, Argentina eventually decided to spurn the IMF negotiating process, opening the door to protracted litigation.

In the lengthy and one-sided debt restructurings that Argentina orchestrated in 2005 and 2010, 91.3% of the defaulted bonds were exchanged for new ones at approximately $0.27-$0.30 on the dollar. Argentina has repudiated bonds not exchanged in an estimated amount of $6.5 billion in principal plus $4.7 billion in past due interest. As of January 2013, holdout bondholder groups (largely hedge funds specializing in distressed sovereign debt) put the total value at some $15 billion with additional past due interest, of which $1.3 billion is in litigation in New York federal court.[45] Although "holdout" bondholders remain unpaid, Argentina is current on its obligations to exchange bondholders, an outcome that is being challenged in court under the equal treatment (*pari passu*) provision of the bonds, which pending a final decision by the appellate court, could force Argentina to find a way to settle with the holdouts in 2013.

The "holdouts" have also lobbied the U.S. government to pressure Argentina to honor its defaulted debt. The Obama Administration invoked financial restrictions against Argentina as defined in U.S. law that include prohibiting official lending and foreign aid and voting against loans to Argentina in the World Bank and the Inter-American Development Bank. In addition, punitive legislation has been introduced in the last three Congresses. Various versions of the Judgment Evading Foreign States Accountability Act cited Argentina for ignoring multiple judgments against it. Its major provisions would have required that such states be labeled "judgment evaders" and that they also be restricted from issuing debt in the United States.

The House Committee on Foreign Affairs, Subcommittee on the Western Hemisphere marked up the bill at the close of the 112th Congress, after which no further action was taken. Opponents of the measure argued that, although sympathetic with the concerns of U.S. stakeholders, the committee lacked jurisdiction, it was imprudent to move ahead while the issue was before federal courts, and that it should be considered in a broader context of U.S.-Argentine relations. To date, similar legislation has not been introduced in Congress and opinions differ as to whether Congress should take a formal position on supporting the holdouts legislatively.[46]

Paris Club Debt

Argentina has also defaulted on bilateral official (government) debt owed to members of the Paris Club, an informal consortium of 19 countries that have agreed to collaborate on a debt workout mechanism to maximize repayment to creditor countries. Congress has authorized the executive branch to negotiate certain debt relief under Paris Club guidelines since 1993 under Foreign Operations Appropriations Acts. This authority covers lending programs such as those under the U.S. Agency for International Development (USAID), military aid programs, the Export-Import Bank, and the Commodity Credit Corporation.[47]

Argentina owes the Paris Club countries $6.3 billion, including $550 to the United States. The Argentine government has twice signaled a desire to address Paris Club debt, but not followed through. Members of Congress have expressed concern over Argentina's failure to resolve this long-standing debt issue, and have supported the Obama Administration's attempts to press the issue with the Argentine government. Argentina could make payments using either its international reserves or current revenue, which some argue it is capable of doing. The Argentine government argues to the contrary. Failure to address this issue is another reason the Obama Administration invoked various financial restrictions on official lending and aid to Argentina.

ICSID Claims

A total of 42 cases claiming $65 billion in damages have been filed against Argentina in the World Bank-sponsored International Centre for Settlement of Investment Disputes (ICSID). ICSID was set up specifically to address grievances taken up under bilateral investment treaties (BITs). Argentina and the United States have had a BIT since 1994. In the 1990s, privatization of state-run agencies became the norm, attracting foreign investment in service industries such as electricity, airlines, and petroleum extraction. Foreign direct investment was further encouraged by the U.S.-Argentina BIT, with net inflows rising rapidly until the crisis. The 2001 financial crisis and changed policy orientation reversed these policies under a public emergency law that eliminated the convertibility regime and allowed the government to renegotiate contracts for utilities. Between frozen utility rates and the huge currency devaluation, foreign investors incurred deep losses, causing them to seek relief at ICSID.[48]

The ICSID panel process is highly complex and rulings on individual cases are not bound by case precedent. This process has led to conflicting opinions, some ruling in favor of plaintiffs, others ruling for Argentina, effectively excusing it from its obligations under the BIT because of the drastic circumstances under which it invoked emergency laws. Given the ICSID process has no appellate review, such inconsistency has caused uncertainty and confusion in the legal community to the point of raising questions over the legitimacy of the ICSID system as it currently operates.[49] In addition, Argentina has taken full advantage of the extensive procedural process, filing for annulments of awards granted by ICSID panels, with both partial and full success in some cases.

In two highly publicized cases, however, ICSID panels awarded specific monetary damages that survived annulment challenges. In September 2007, an ICSID panel ruled in favor of CMS Gas Transmission Company of Michigan for operating losses incurred from the emergency laws and regulations, awarding $132 million in damages. In September 2009, another panel found in favor of Azurix Corporation (water and sewer contract) for $165 million.[50] In a controversial stance, Argentina has declined to pay any ICSID awards, in part over fear of setting a precedent that could be costly given the many cases filed against it in ICSID. Among the tactics it has adopted is to interpret Articles 53 and 54 of the 1965 ICSID Convention as allowing Argentina to require that plaintiff submit its judgment award to an Argentine court for final settlement.[51] Argentina has applied this rationale to both U.S. cases, among others where damages have been awarded, but the United States and many other countries do not recognize this line of reasoning.[52]

Legal representatives of the Argentine government have further stated that it will continue to refute ICSID claims and consider taking the additional step of adopting legislation that would annul most of its bilateral investment treaties as unconstitutional.[53] In response, and at the request of U.S. claimants, the Obama Administration on March 26, 2012, decided to suspend Argentina from tariff preferences provided under the U.S. Generalized System of Preferences (GSP).[54] In 2011, 11% of U.S. imports from Argentina entered duty free under GSP.

Nationalizations and Expropriations

Part of the Argentine economic strategy since 2001 has been to reassert government control over a select group of firms, essentially expropriating and nationalizing their assets. This has applied to both Argentine and foreign firms. As discussed above, Argentina nationalized private pension funds in 2008 in order to expand the government financial assets and took over Aerolineas Argentinas, which was partially owned by a group of Spanish investors.

On April 16, 2012, Argentina initiated the renationalization of Yacimientos Petrolifero Fiscales (YPF), the largest oil company in Argentina. It produces one-third of national crude output and half of refined fuel. YPF was organized in 1922 under state control, where it remained until privatized in 1992. The nationalization was accomplished by legislation calling for the expropriation of controlling interest of the 57% ownership by Spanish firm Reposol. The government argued that a decline in oil production had negative effects on tax revenue and raised the cost of energy subsidies, which had to be continued with high-priced foreign imports, further hurting the trade balance. In addition, lower oil production threatened Argentina's goal of energy self-sufficiency. Argentina, however, has long thought of YPF as a source of public revenue and energy self-sufficiency. Its long history of state control also created a strong national brand identity that may have played a part in the broad public approval of its renationalization in 2012.[55]

Opponents of the expropriation argue that government policies played critical roles in the decline of oil production that actually began in 1998. After the 2001 financial crisis, the government introduced oil export taxes and oil price controls in 2006, reducing the YPF profitability and competiveness of

Argentine energy exports. These measures directly affected YPF's profitability and incentives to invest and produce. In effect, they argue that the Argentine government set up YPF to fail, and thereby orchestrated the conditions that would justify its nationalization.[56] The settlement issue remains unresolved and has caused a severe deterioration in relations between Spain and Argentina. It has also raised the question of whether other firms may be at risk.

Trade Protectionism

Argentina practices an increasingly complex strategy of trade protectionism, largely to support macroeconomic goals. Relatively high tariffs, import restrictions, export taxes, and limits on foreign exchange transactions are all employed to manage the current account balance, prices and supplies of consumption goods, and political support. The Global Trade Alert, in its most recent annual report, notes that Argentina and China are the only two countries in the world that are in the top 10 list of offenders for all four major categories of discriminatory harm it measures by the number of (1) discriminatory measures, (2) tariff lines, (3) sectors affected, and (4) trading partners involved. Argentina is at the top of the list globally for most sectors affected by protectionist measures.[57] The WTO cites similar problems in a recent trade policy review.[58]

The Office of the United States Trade Representative (USTR) lists a host of discriminatory import practices affecting U.S. exporters that include high import duties. The WTO indicates that 27% of Argentina's import tariff lines have average applied tariffs exceeding 15%, with 4% of tariff lines having a tariff of 35%. Textiles, clothing, footwear, and oil seeds are the most protected sectors.[59] In addition there are or have been numerous nontariff barriers including automatic and nonautomatic licensing requirements, port-of-entry restrictions, cumbersome customs procedures and documentation, and restrictions on imports of used capital goods. Exceptions are given for specific goods when viewed in the national interest of Argentina, but many import restrictions are not codified and are apparently applied in an arbitrary fashion. Many restrictions are openly applied to protect domestic industries and promote local production. These affect many of the major U.S. export categories including metallurgical products, automotive parts, chemical products, and general purpose machinery.[60]

The United States, the European Union (EU), and Japan filed dispute settlement cases against Argentina in the World Trade Organization (WTO) on

December 6, 2012, challenging Argentina's non-automatic licensing policies, and government requests that firms balance imports into Argentina with exports, or make investments of equal value in productive operations. In response, Argentina repealed the non-automatic licenses on January 25, 2013. The WTO agreed on January 28, 2013, to establish a dispute panel nonetheless. Plaintiffs argued that the problem was not fully addressed and that additional information was necessary to resolve the issue.

Although Argentina lifted the non-automatic licensing requirement, it simultaneously raised tariff levels to 35% on 100 other products and retains a cumbersome automatic import licensing regime. In retaliation, Argentina requested and secured a WTO dispute panel on the same day to rule on its complaint that U.S. restrictions on Argentine beef are contrary to WTO rules. Argentina also has a complaint against Spain, which is blocking imports of biodiesel fuel in retaliation for the nationalization of YPF.[61]

Exports are also controlled to meet broader economic objectives. In particular, there are high export taxes on hydrocarbon and agricultural commodities, often pricing raw exports higher than processed goods, encouraging value-added production in Argentina. Soybean exports are taxed at 35%, wheat at 23%, and corn at 20%. In addition, there are also cumbersome export registration procedures in some cases, with government policy openly delaying or denying shipping to meet domestic price and supply needs. For example, the Argentine government imposed wheat quotas in 2006, adjusting the level periodically to meet domestic needs. In June 2012 it increased the quota to appease farmers and increase government revenue. By December 2012, the quota had again been adjusted downward because a low harvest threatened prescribed domestic price and supply levels. These policies resulted in strikes and protests by farmers in 2012 over export quotas, high export taxes, and administrative costs.[62]

In addition to domestic resistance, Argentina's trade policies have brought retaliation from countries around the world. In April 2012, 40 members of the WTO, including the United States, denounced Argentina at a WTO meeting for the rise of protectionist practices. On May 25, 2012, the EU took the next step and filed a suit against Argentina in the WTO over its import restrictions for being inconsistent with international trade rules.[63]

Capital and Currency Controls

Since the financial crisis, Argentina made a sustained effort to build up its international reserves. From 2002 to 2010, these rose from $10.4 billion to $52.2 billion. As confidence in the economy and policies of the Fernández government began to slide, capital began to exit the country, as evidenced by the $6 billion decline in reserves in 2011, followed by a $1 billion fall in 2012 to $40.5 billion as of March 27, 2013. The government countered by tightening capital controls in 2011 to increase dollar inflows and stem capital flight through forced repatriation of export revenue and investments by mining and insurance companies (requiring conversion to pesos), restrictions on the purchase of foreign currency, the addition of fees on use of credit cards in foreign countries, the imposition of import controls, and reserve requirements on certain foreign investment. As discussed earlier, there may be reason to question, given recent trends, whether the reserve level is sufficient to maintain confidence in the peso.[64]

U.S. and other foreign investors and firms operating in Argentina are hurt by these restrictions and requirements, and some may be challengeable under the U.S.-Argentina BIT rules that govern free movement of capital.[65] Continued restrictions on the exchange rate may provide temporary relief, but ultimately the real appreciation of the peso suggests limited opportunity for a soft correction and increased probability of a major devaluation at some point. Such a policy environment further entices the movement from pesos to dollars and Euros, continued capital flight, and relatively weaker foreign investment in the future, compounding Argentina's problems.

IMF Reporting Requirements and Article IV Reviews

Under the Articles of Agreement of the IMF, member countries are required to meet high standards in economic data reporting and submit to Article IV reviews of their economy. Argentina has failed to meet both of these requirements. Inflation reporting has been discredited since 2007, and GDP figures more recently. Argentina has been further criticized for fining and harassing independent economists who have seen fit to produce their own inflation statistics. Argentina has failed to submit to an Article IV review since 2006. The IMF has warned Argentina that its membership in the institution may be at risk if it does not accommodate requests to conform to IMF requirements by September 30, 2013. On February 1, 2013, the IMF issued a formal declaration of censure to Argentina for failure to live up to its obligations under the Articles of Agreement and gave Argentina until September 29, 2013, to upgrade data reporting. The Managing Director is scheduled to issue a status report to the Executive Board by November 13, 2013.[66]

OUTLOOK

Argentina's economic policies reflect a certain distrust of international institutions and the government's priority for financial independence, social equity, and what may be considered a commitment to "populist" solutions. This review of these economic policies is not meant to suggest that there is one ideal macroeconomic model that is being violated. Rather, even in recognizing that countries can govern themselves well under alternative policy frameworks and priorities, what stands out for many in the case of Argentina is the sense that policy choices have introduced major distortions in the economy and that deteriorating external accounts, among other factors, are increasing the risk of financial crisis, particularly if history is any judge. Trade protection, managed exchange rates, and capital controls are policy adjustments required to address problems that materialize in a constrained economic system (e.g., subsidy-driven fiscal expansion, price controls, inability to borrow internationally) that cannot easily accommodate current account deficits, a market exchange rate, or standard macroeconomic responses to combat high inflation.

Among the more obvious policy corrections would be to introduce more flexibility in the exchange rate, ease away from an expansionist monetary policy, and begin correcting fiscal deficits. In their absence, Argentina increases the risk of eventually experiencing a more serious economic adjustment. It may be premature, however, to foretell the demise of the Argentine economy. Despite increasing bottlenecks, thresholds that predict collapse so far appear not to have been breached for inflation, current account and fiscal balances, or debt, and Argentina has shown a proclivity for surviving economically. The expected strong soy crop for 2013 and absence of external shocks may allow the Argentine government to continue with the current economic program for some time.

Even if there were a desire for a policy correction in Buenos Aires, however, it could be difficult to implement and still avoid a "hard landing" and attendant political and social ramifications. In fact, it may be that a change in policy toward foreign stakeholders will not occur until either a new government takes office, a new crisis erupts in the wake of large and unsustainable macroeconomic distortions, or both.

International stakeholders, both public and private, find themselves challenged by this system, along with many Argentines. Stakeholders, including the United States, criticize Argentina for eschewing standard norms of economic behavior and the rule of law, and in response, have sought remedy in national courts and international arbitration, eliminated financial and trade benefits, and previously introduced hardline legislative resolutions. One indication of the breadth of dissatisfaction over Argentina's policies is the call for effectively removing Argentina from the G-20, despite the lack of precedent and formal procedure for doing this. Notwithstanding these initiatives, Argentina has not been moved to change course, and Congress may decide to consider once again U.S. options for addressing bilateral concerns with Argentina.

End Notes

[1] Foreign direct investment data are available at the U.S. Department of Commerce, Bureau of Economic Analysis (BEA) at http://www.bea.gov/international/index.htm.

[2] Greece has technically exceeded Argentina as the largest sovereign default, but without the prolonged acrimony. For details on Argentina's default, see CRS Report R41029, Argentina's Defaulted Sovereign Debt: Dealing with the "Holdouts," by J. F. Hornbeck.

[3] The term "populist" is admittedly a controversial and, for some, a pejorative term. It, nonetheless, has a fairly well-established understanding in Latin American economic history. This report focuses on the populism of macroeconomic policy, which may be defined as "an approach to economics that emphasizes growth and income redistribution and deemphasizes the risks of inflation and deficit finance, external constraints, and the reaction of economic agents to aggressive nonmarket policies." This definition is not meant to diminish in any way the legitimate concern for distributional issues in economic policy, but serves as a type of unifying understanding of policies that historically, often have not ended well for those very groups such policies are intended to benefit. See, Rudiger Dornbusch and Sebastian Edwards, "The Macroeconomics of Populism," in The Macroeconomics of Populism in Latin America, ed. Rudiger Dornbusch and Sebastian Edwards (Chicago: University of Chicago Press, 1991), pp. 7-15.

[4] From 2003 through 2011, the value of Argentina's soy exports to China (the primary export) rose by 241%, reflecting a 43% rise in volume and 138% increase in price. Similar trends occurred for the other two major exports, soy oil and crude petroleum. Dependence on commodity trade is not new. As one long-time historian of Argentina commented on its economic status in the 19th century, "Prosperity based on good harvests and strong overseas markets obscured a dangerous vulnerability," namely, the eventuality of a sudden fall in prices and increase in imports that leads to current account and debt problems. Colin M. MacLachlan, Argentina: What Went Wrong (Westport: Praeger, 2006), p. 36.

[5] Universidad Torcuarto Di Tella, Indice de Confianza en el Gobierno, http://www.utdt.edu.

[6] As quoted from the Banco Central de la República, Inflation Report Second Quarter 2012, May 2012, p. 59 and Macroeconomic and Monetary Policy Report, July 2012, p. 6. Interviews with government officials at the Ministry of Foreign Relations and Ministry of Economy and Public Finance in Buenos Aires September 2012 reinforced this priority.

[7] In fact, electricity is provided at a fraction of its cost and all forms of public transit (buses, subway, commuter trains), cost no more than US$0.50 to ride. There are also subsidies in the tax code for families, which reportedly increased some 26% in 2012. IHS Global Insight, Subsidies Increased in Argentina, Low Official Inflation Rate Unchanged, September 17, 2012.

[8] La Nación, February 4 and 19, 2013.

[9] Fundación de Investigaciones Economicas Latinoamericanas, (FIEL), power point presentation, La Economía Argentina: Situación Actual y Perspectivas, September 2012.

[10] INDEC, Nota de Prensa, Las Remuneraciones en la Industria Manufacturera Aumentaron un 7.2% durante el Tercer Trimestre del Año, October 31, 2012, and FIEL, ibid.

[11] FIEL, ibid.

[12] Some now refer to the effects of the extended commodity boom as the "Milagro Argentino," or Argentine miracle.

[13] Discussions at the Universidad del CEMA, Buenos Aires, September 2012.

[14] World Trade Organization, Argentina Trade Policy Review Report, WTO Secretariat, WT/TPR/S/227, February 13, 2013, p. ix.

[15] It is perhaps a bit ironic that this government-owned bank was created in 1891 out of the ashes of its predecessor, the Banco Nacional, after the former failed trying to service short-term government debt owed to Europe, see MacLachlan, Argentina: What Went Wrong, p. 38.

[16] Banco Central de la República, Inflation Report Second Quarter 2012, May 2012, p. 54, and Financial Stability Report: Second Half 2012, October 2012, pp. 39-40.

[17] Ibid.

[18] Argentina defaulted three times on its domestic debt between 1980 and 2001. See, Carmen M. Reinhart and Kenneth S. Rogoff, This Time Is Different: Eight Centuries of Financial Folly, (Princeton: Princeton University Press, 2009), p. 111.

[19] Business Monitor International, Latin America Monitor: Southern Cone, March 2013.

[20] Banco Central de la República Argentina, Argentina: Macroeconomic, Monetary, and Financial Outlook, Power Point Presentation, Buenos Aires, August 2012, p. 62.

[21] Ibid., p. 58.

[22] Banco Central de la República, Inflation Report Second Quarter 2012, p. 59-60 and United Nations, Economic Commission on Latin America and the Caribbean, Macroeconomic Report on Latin America and the Caribbean, Washington, D.C., June 2012, pp. 70-72.

[23] Given Argentina's inability to borrow internationally and the decline in foreign investment, the other major sources of dollars come from exports, export taxes, and forced repatriation of profits.

[24] This level of reserves equals approximately 7 months of imports for 2012, considered more than sufficient to cover balance of payments needs by "conventional" standards. In a country with capital, export, and import controls, as well as a managed exchange rate, indications of capital flight, and a steady decline in reserves, it is less than clear that this is an adequate backstop. See, IMF, Assessing the Need for Foreign Currency Reserves, http://www.imf.org/external/ pubsft/survey/so/2011/POL040711B.htm.

[25] Eliana Raszewski, "Disappearing Dollars Compound Default Threat: Argentina Credit," Bloomberg, February 28, 2013.

[26] BCRA, Inflation Report, pp. 59-60. The financial instruments in question are Letras del Banco Central (LEBACs), which can be issued with short-, medium-, and long-term maturities, and Notas del Banco Central (NOBACs), or medium-term notes or bonds. Both are auctioned regularly and trade in the secondary market. The BCRA may issue them as needed given the ability to sell at will to agencies of the federal government.

[27] BCRA, Ibid., pp. 59-60. In Argentina, M2 = cash + checking deposits + savings deposits. M3 adds certificates of deposit (CDs).

[28] The Economist, Official Statistics: Don't Lie to Me, Argentina, February 25, 2012.

[29] INDEC, Nota de Prensa, Las Remuneraciones en la Industria Manufacturera Aumentaron un 7.2% durante el Tercer Trimestre del Año, October 31, 2012, Banco Central de la República Argentina, Argentina: Macroeconomic, Monetary, and Financial Outlook, and Inflation Report, pp. 67 and 72.

[30] See, Alberto Cavallo, "Online and Official Price Indexes: Measuring Argentina's Inflation," Journal of Monetary Economics, vol. 60, no. 1 and http://www.InflacionVerdadera.com.

[31] Paula Diosquez, Argentina: Country Intelligence Report, IHS Global Insight, August 24, 2012, p. 9.

[32] Cavallo, op. cit., p. 12.

[33] BCRA, Inflation Report, p. 63.

[34] Banco Central de la República Argentina, Financial Stability Report: Second Half 2012, October 2012, pp. 39-40. Global Insight, December 2012, p. 11.

[35] Ibid., p. 59.

[36] BCRA, Macroeconomic and Monetary Policy Report, pp. 5-6.

[37] Banco Central de la República Argentina, Argentina: Macroeconomic, Monetary, and Financial Outlook, Power Point Presentation, Buenos Aires, September 2012, p. 70.

[38] Ibid.

[39] Reinhart and Rogoff, This Time Is Different: Eight Centuries of Financial Folly, pp. 106, 111, 117, and 143, and Alan M. Taylor, "Capital Accumulation," in A New Economic History of Argentina, ed. Gerardo della Paolera and Alan M. Taylor (Cambridge: Cambridge University Press, 2005), pp. 340-346.

[40] Banco Central de la Republica Argentina, Argentina: Macroeconomic RADAR, updated March 15, 2013.

[41] The extent of the peso's possible overvaluation is subject to debate. The dollar exchange rate may not be the most relevant. Argentina trades more with Brazil than the United States, which suggests the Brazilian real would be a more relevant comparison, and for which there is a smaller differential. A basket of currencies yields a similar result, suggesting to many that there may still be room for appreciation in the Argentine peso. The government argues there is no strong evidence of an overvalued peso. Nonetheless, the pure arbitrage opportunities and exchange rate controls point to some significant degree of exchange rate misalignment, which is worsening.

[42] Latin America Monitor, Southern Cone, April 2013, p. 3. In countries with high inflation, distortions like parallel exchange rates and exchange controls can be "the norm," as pointed out in Reinhart and Rogoff, This Time Is Different: Eight Centuries of Financial Folly, pp. 193.

[43] MacLachlan, Argentina: What Went Wrong, p.189.

[44] This is a short summary of a complex issue. For details on the default, see CRS Report R41029, Argentina's Defaulted Sovereign Debt: Dealing with the "Holdouts," by J. F. Hornbeck.

[45] Robert J. Shapiro, Decision Time for Argentina, congressional staff meeting, December 6, 2012, and SEC Form 18- K, p. 140.

[46] U.S. Congress, House Committee on Foreign Affairs, Markup Before the Subcommittee on the Western Hemisphere on H.R. 1798 Judgment Evading Foreign States Accountability Act of 2011, 112th Congress, 2d sess., November 29, 2012, Serial No. 112-188, (Washington: GPO, 2012), p. 38.

[47] CRS Report RS21482, The Paris Club and International Debt Relief, by Martin A. Weiss.

[48] Eric David Kasenetz, "Desperate Times Call for Desperate Measures: The Aftermath of Argentina's State of Necessity and the Current Fight in the ICSID," George Washington International Law Review, vol. 41 (714), January 2011.

[49] Ibid., pp. 724-27 and 733-735. This discussion does not constitute a legal analysis of the cases, but presents only a summary of key points.

[50] Case summaries are available at https://icsid.worldbank.org/ICSID/Index.jsp.

[51] SEC, Form 18-K, pp. 189-190.

[52] Kasenetz, op. cit., pp. 740-741.

[53] MercoPress, South Atlantic News Agency, Argentina Faces 65bn Dollars in Claims; Plans to Abandon International Litigations Court, November 28, 2012.

[54] The Economist, Come and Get Me: Argentina Is Putting International Arbitration to the Test, February 18, 2012.

[55] Martin Castellano, Ramon Aracena, and Todd Martinez. Argentina: Chronicle of a Nationalization Foretold, Institute of International Finance, April 23, 2012, and MacLauchlan, Argentina: What Went Wrong, p. 84.

[56] Ibid.

[57] Simon J. Evenett, ed., Debacle: The 11th Global Trade Act Report on Protectionism, Global Trade Alert, Centre for Economic Policy Research, London, June 2012, p. 6.

[58] WTO, Argentina Trade Policy Review Report, p. xi-xii.

[59] Ibid.

[60] Ibid and Office of the United States Trade Representative, 2012 National Trade Estimate Report on Foreign Trade Barriers, Washington, D.C., March 2012.

[61] http://www.wto.org/english/news_e/news13_e/dsb_28jan13_e.htm, David Haskel, "Argentina Lifts Some Import Restraints, But Imposes Maximum Duties on 100 Items," International Trade Reporter, and Daniel Pruzin, "U.S., EU, Japan Secure WTO Panel To Rule on Argentine Import Restrictions," International Trade Reporter, Bloomberg BNA, January 31, 2013.

[62] The Wall Street Journal, Argentina Cuts 2012-14 Wheat Export Quota, December 10, 2012, IHS Global Insight, Argentine Government Lifts Ceiling on Wheat Exports, June 25, 2012, David Haskel, "Argentine Farmers' Strike Goes Nationwide, Temporarily Halts Grain, Soybean Deliveries," International Trade Reporter, Bloomberg BNA, June 14, 2012.

[63] Ken Parks, "Argentina Challenges U.S. Ban on Its Beef," Wall Street Journal, September 1-2, 2012, International Trade Daily, April 2, 2012, and Washington Trade Daily, May 30, 2012.

[64] USTR, 2012 Foreign Trade Barriers and IMF, Global Markets Monitor, February 17, 2012.

[65] Ibid.

[66] International Monetary Fund, Statement by the IMF Executive Board on Argentina, Press Release No. 13/33, February 1, 2013.

In: Argentina
Editor: Eileen Mckinney

ISBN: 978-1-63482-251-0

Chapter 3

ARGENTINA 2013 HUMAN RIGHTS REPORT*

U.S. Department of State;
Bureau of Democracy, Human Rights and Labor

EXECUTIVE SUMMARY

Argentina is a federal constitutional republic. Cristina Fernandez de Kirchner won re-election to the presidency in October 2011 in multi-party elections the media and various nongovernmental organizations (NGOs) described as generally free and fair. The country also held legislative midterm elections on October 27. Security forces reported to civilian authorities but occasionally acted at lower levels independently of civilian control and committed human rights abuses.

The principal human rights problems included reports of torture by provincial police, harsh prison conditions, and gender violence.

Other human rights problems included use of excessive force by police; occasional arbitrary arrest and detention; prolonged pretrial detention; actions that risked impairing freedom of the press; continued concerns about judicial inefficiency; official corruption; child abuse; continuing discrimination against and infringements on the rights of indigenous people; sex trafficking; forced labor, primarily within the country; and child labor.

---

* This is an edited, reformatted and augmented version of a report issued by the U.S. Department of State; Bureau of Democracy, Human Rights and Labor, March 2014.

Judicial authorities prosecuted a number of officials who committed abuses during the year; however, some officials engaged in corruption or other abuses with impunity.

Section 1. Respect for the Integrity of the Person, Including Freedom From

a. Arbitrary or Unlawful Deprivation of Life

There were reports of deaths as a result of the police's use of unwarranted or excessive force. Federal security forces have the authority to conduct internal investigations into alleged abuses and to fire individuals who have allegedly committed a human rights violation.

On September 30, two policemen from the metropolitan police and Buenos Aires province police force shot and killed a 29-year-old man after an argument. The security secretary asserted that one of the policemen intentionally fired his weapon, and remanded the case to the judge to investigate.

The NGO Coordinator Against Police Repression (CORREPI) reported in July that security forces using excessive force killed 56 persons during the first half of the year. The Center for Legal and Social Studies (CELS) reported deaths as a result of police using unwarranted or excessive force in the city of Buenos Aires and Buenos Aires Province during the first half of the year.

b. Disappearance

There were no reports of politically motivated disappearances.

Authorities continued to investigate and prosecute individuals implicated in disappearances, killings, and torture committed during the 1976-83 military dictatorship (widely referred to as the "Dirty War"). Investigations into the "systematic plan" of the military dictatorship, including the appropriation of children of detainees and the killing of detainees on "death flights," continued or began during the year. CELS estimated that 381 judicial investigations were active by May, in which 2,088 persons were charged for crimes against humanity. According to the Attorney General's Office for Follow-up on Crimes Against Humanity, from January to October the courts convicted 76 individuals for committing human rights abuses during the 1976-83 period and continued trials that were suspended in 1989-90 when the government issued a blanket pardon. For example, in September a criminal court of appeals upheld a conviction for the torture and murder of Carlos Moreno, a union representative and worker at the Loma Negra company. The tribunal sentenced three former army officials and two civilians to prison for their involvement in the case, ruling for the first time since these cases resumed that civilians had participated in crimes against humanity.

Judicial authorities continued to investigate cases of kidnapping and illegal adoption of children born to detained dissidents by members of the former military dictatorship. In April a judge sentenced a couple who illegally adopted the son of a disappeared family to six years in prison. The individual who illegally offered the baby to the couple also faced charges for identity theft. The NGO Abuelas de la Plaza de Mayo reported the number of persons illegally adopted by former military officials and later identified and made aware of their background increased to 109 of an estimated 500 born to detained and missing dissidents during the former military dictatorship.

The Argentine Forensic Anthropology Team (EAAF) continued cooperation with the government in the identification of remains of Dirty War victims. In August the National Institute of Industrial Technology (INTI) and the EAAF signed an agreement for INTI to provide technical support and assistance to the EAAF.

c. Torture and Other Cruel, Inhuman, or Degrading Treatment or Punishment

The law prohibits torture and other cruel, inhuman, or degrading treatment or punishment and provides penalties for torture similar to those for homicide. Nevertheless, international organizations, CELS, the Office of the National Public Prosecutor, and the Buenos Aires Provincial Memory Commission's Committee Against Torture (an autonomous office established by the provincial government) reported complaints of torture perpetrated by provincial and federal prison officials.

In September members of the Coordination and Follow-up System of Penitentiaries--a federal system with representatives from the Criminal Superior Tribunal, the General Prosecutor's Office, the National Defender's Office, the Federal Penitentiary, and CELS--visited various federal prisons. Their findings prompted the closure of some areas of Marcos Paz Penitentiary in Buenos Aires Province, where cells lacked electricity and bathrooms, and prisoners waited up to three months for access to shower facilities.

According to the 2012 annual report of the Buenos Aires Provincial Memory Commission's Committee Against Torture, deficiencies in food or health care and practices such as beatings, threats, and forced isolation remained common in prisons in the province of Buenos Aires. The report of the April 2012 prison visits of the UN special rapporteur on torture was not available by December.

Prison and Detention Center Conditions

Prison conditions often were harsh. Inmates in many facilities suffered from extreme overcrowding, poor nutrition, inadequate medical and psychological treatment, inadequate sanitation, limited family visits, and frequent degrading treatment, according to various reports by human rights organizations and research centers.

Physical Conditions: The number of prisoners in Buenos Aires provincial penitentiaries was approximately 30,000 and exceeded facility capacity by an estimated 92 percent, according to a 2010 report by the provincial Council of Defenders. Prison capacity in federal penitentiaries was adequate, according to the Federal Penitentiary Service, with slightly more than 9,800 inmates in federal prisons and more than 10,900 beds.

Authorities held women separately from men, and the law permits children to stay in prison with their mothers until the age of four. According to the Federal Penitentiary Service, 785 women were in federal prisons. Women constituted 8 percent of the overall prison population. CELS estimated that 60 percent of the women incarcerated in Buenos Aires provincial prisons were in pretrial detention or awaiting sentencing, and many were held with convicted prisoners. In general men's prisons were more violent, dangerous, and crowded than women's prisons.

Overcrowding in juvenile facilities often resulted in minors being held in police station facilities, even though some NGOs and the national prison ombudsman warned the law prohibited doing so.

NGOs and media reports alleged poor prison conditions in several provinces. On April 14, a fire in a prison in the city of Rosario killed three prisoners and injured seven others. The lead prosecutor at the General Prosecutor's Office of Institutional Violence described current prison conditions as a "constant and massive violation of human rights" affecting 60,000 to 65,000 detainees.

Prisoners received potable water.

Administration: Information on the adequacy of recordkeeping and alternatives to sentencing for nonviolent offenders was unavailable. Prisoners and detainees generally had access to visitors and could observe their religious practices. Authorities permitted prisoners and detainees to submit complaints to judicial authorities without censorship and to request investigation of credible allegations of inhumane conditions. Some local NGOs noted, however, that access to a public defender was sometimes limited and that prisoners occasionally did not submit complaints to authorities due to fear of reprisal.

In August the national director of the Federal Penitentiary Service, Victor Hortel, resigned following complaints of alleged official complicity after 13 high-risk prisoners escaped from Ezeiza Penitentiary by digging a tunnel and breaking four boundary fences.

Independent Monitoring: The government permitted independent prison visits by local and international human rights observers, and such visits took place during the year.

d. Arbitrary Arrest or Detention

The law prohibits arbitrary arrest and detention, and the government generally observed these prohibitions; however, police reportedly arrested and detained citizens arbitrarily on occasion.

Role of the Police and Security Apparatus

The federal police normally have jurisdiction for maintaining law and order in the federal capital and for federal crimes in the provinces. Other federal police authorities include the airport security police, Gendarmerie, Coast Guard, and Bureau of Prisons. All federal police forces fall under the authority of the Security Ministry. Each province and the city of Buenos Aires also has its own police force that responds to a provincial (or city) security ministry or secretariat. Individual forces varied considerably in their effectiveness and respect for human rights. In late August, as a measure to combat growing insecurity, Security Minister Arturo Puricelli dispatched 5,000 additional Gendarmerie officers to assume urban policing duties in the province of Buenos Aires. In order to avoid leaving the borders unprotected, the army agreed to send soldiers to cooperate with the Gendarmerie in the border area with Brazil and Uruguay.

Federal security forces have the authority to conduct internal investigations into alleged abuses and to fire individuals who have allegedly committed a human rights violation. The federal government can also file complaints with the federal courts, and provincial governments can do the same for provincial security forces.

Members of security forces convicted of a crime were subject to stiff penalties. Generally authorities administratively suspended officers accused of wrongdoing until their investigations were completed. Authorities investigated and in some cases detained, prosecuted, and convicted the officers involved.

Arrest Procedures and Treatment of Detainees

Police generally apprehended individuals openly with warrants based on sufficient evidence and issued by a duly authorized official. Police may detain suspects for up to 10 hours without an arrest warrant if authorities have a well-founded belief that the suspects have committed or are about to commit a crime, or police are unable to determine the suspect's identity. Human rights groups reported police occasionally arrested persons arbitrarily and detained suspects longer than 10 hours.

The law provides a detainee with the right to a prompt determination of the legality of the detention by a lower criminal court judge, who determines whether to proceed with an investigation. In some cases there were delays in this process and in informing detainees of the charges against them.

The law provides for the right to bail except in cases involving narcotics, violent crimes, and firearms violations.

Authorities allowed detainees prompt access to counsel and provided public defenders in cases where they were unable to afford counsel. In some cases such access was delayed due to an overburdened system.

Pretrial Detention: The law provides for investigative detention of up to two years for indicted persons awaiting or undergoing trial; the period may be extended by one year in limited circumstances. The slow pace of the justice system often resulted in lengthy detentions beyond the period stipulated by law. According to statistics from the Federal Penitentiary Service, more than 5,400 detainees (of 9,800 prisoners) in federal prisons were in pretrial detention, awaiting sentencing, or awaiting the appeals process. According to several human rights organizations, 30 percent of pretrial detainees were eventually acquitted. A convicted prisoner usually receives credit for time already served.

e. Denial of Fair Public Trial

The law provides for the right to a fair trial, and the independent judiciary generally enforced this right. Judicial scholars continued to report inefficiencies and delays in the judicial system, and Chief Justice Lorenzetti asked criminal judges to speed up proceedings. According to some local NGOs, judges in some federal criminal and ordinary courts were subject occasionally to political manipulation.

Delays, procedural logjams, long gaps in the appointment of judges, inadequate administrative support, and general inefficiency hampered the judicial system. NGOs also criticized all three branches of the government for inefficiencies in the process for selecting judges. Judges' broad discretion on whether and how to pursue investigations contributed to a public perception that many decisions were arbitrary.

In May the National Congress approved a six-part presidential judicial reform project, including a Council of Magistrates reform law. In June the Supreme Court ruled four articles of the law unconstitutional, striking down a provision to select new judges by popular election, stating it disrupted the institution's balance of power and challenged judicial independence. In early May the UN special rapporteur on the independence of judges and lawyers expressed concern over parts of the project.

Trial Procedures

Trials are public. In federal and provincial courts, defendants enjoy a presumption of innocence and have the right to appeal, have legal counsel, and call defense witnesses. If needed, a public defender is provided at public expense when defendants face serious criminal charges. During the investigative stage, defendants can submit questions in writing to the investigating judge. A panel of judges decides guilt or innocence. Although defendants and their attorneys have access to government-held evidence, local NGOs indicated that defendants sometimes experienced obstacles or delays in obtaining such evidence. Defendants can present witnesses and provide expert witness reports, in addition to the defendant's own evidence. Lengthy delays in trials occurred nationwide, with many cases taking five or more years to resolve.

Federal and provincial courts continued the transition to trials with oral arguments in criminal cases, replacing the old system of written submissions. Although the 1994 constitution provides for trial by jury, implementing legislation was not passed by November. In Cordoba Province, however, defendants accused of certain serious crimes have the right to a trial by jury, and the province of Buenos Aires passed similar legislation in September.

An unofficially organized juvenile justice system operated in eight of 18 districts in Buenos Aires Province. It provides minors between the ages of 16 and 18 with the same procedural rights as adults and limits sentences to 180 days in prison.

Political Prisoners and Detainees

There were no reports of political prisoners or detainees.

Civil Judicial Procedures and Remedies

Citizens have access to the courts to bring lawsuits seeking damages or the protection of rights provided by the constitution. Local observers criticized various interested parties, including the government, for seeking to pressure judges and shape judicial outcomes to benefit the government.

Regional Human Rights Court Decisions

The country is subject to the jurisdiction of the Inter-American Court of Human Rights. In May the court ordered the country to reform the juvenile justice system to adhere to regional and international human rights conventions to avoid violating minor prisoners' human rights.

f. Arbitrary Interference with Privacy, Family, Home, or Correspondence

The constitution prohibits such actions, and the government generally respected these prohibitions.

In late April Cordoba Province police attempted without a warrant to evict 60 families squatting on vacantproperty.

Section 2. Respect for Civil Liberties, Including

a. Freedom of Speech and Press

The constitution provides for freedom of speech and press; the government generally respected these rights. Independent newspapers, radio and television outlets, and internet sites were numerous and active, expressing a wide variety of views. Private media outlets were independent from the national and provincial governments.

Press Freedoms: All major supermarket and home appliance retailers ceased advertising in newspapers in February. Although retailers privately claimed the Domestic Trade Secretariat ordered this action to weaken independent media companies, no retailers publicly made this claim, which the government denied. While the limitation was in place, paid advertising decreased an estimated 70 percent, which organizations such as the Inter American Press Association (IAPA), the International Association of Broadcasting, and the Argentine Association of News Organizations cited as endangering press freedom through economic damage. The Consumers Union of Argentina launched a campaign protesting the ban on advertising. In July the government sanctioned the organization for misusing public funds to defend private media companies. Following changes in personnel at the federal level, including a new secretary of domestic commerce, there were indications near the end of the year that the restrictions had been lifted. In December many supermarkets resumed buying advertising in print and audiovisual news media.

Despite previous Supreme Court rulings ordering the government to apply reasonable balance in the distribution of public advertising, placement of official advertising remained arbitrary. In 2012 media outlets critical of the government received a disproportionately small fraction of the total public advertising budget. Official data showed that media groups close to the government obtained more than 45 percent of public advertising from 2009 to 2012. The two newspapers with the highest circulation and both critical of the government received less than 1 percent of the total public advertising budget. During the year the government agreed to abide by a 2009 federal appeals court ruling that withholding government advertising from Editorial Perfil outlets generally critical of the government violated freedom of the press as guaranteed in the constitution. As of October, however, the amount of public advertising in Editorial Perfil outlets was only between 7 percent and 16 percent of court-ordered levels.

The Supreme Court ruled in favor of the constitutionality of a media law passed in 2009 but still not fully implemented. On November 4, Clarin Group presented a voluntary divestment plan to comply with the law, which remained under government study in December.

Violence and Harassment: The Argentine Journalism Forum, an NGO promoting freedom of expression, reported 152 attacks on freedom of expression between January and September, up 32 percent from the same period in 2012.

On April 26, Buenos Aires city police agents attacked a group of 11 journalists and photographers from different media outlets who were covering a union protest at Borda mental health hospital. Police arrested one journalist and injured several others with rubber bullets. In reporting the Borda incident and two other capital city police attacks on journalists, CELs concluded that repeated attacks on journalists visibly carrying microphones or cameras in their hands seemed intended to prevent the recording and reporting of violent actions by police personnel.

On August18, following a television report by Clarin Group journalist Jorge Lanata on cases of alleged corruption, the secretary general of the presidency, Oscar Parrilli, issued a press release calling Lanata "a contract killer hired by Magnetto" (Clarin Group's chief executive officer) and asserting his objective was to "spread hate" against President Cristina Kirchner. Parrilli subsequently added during a radio interview that Lanata was a "killer operating in the media." IAPA criticized those comments, warning they could trigger "more attacks against journalists."

Censorship or Content Restrictions: In August public television Channel 7 removed news anchor Juan Miceli from its daily news broadcast after an interview in which his questioning upset a ruling party congressperson. Other Channel 7 programs subsequently discredited Miceli, who was eventually dismissed.

Actions to Expand Press Freedom

The Supreme Court ruled in favor of a blogger being sued by a public university official for defamation, stating that opinions on the internet are protected by the same rights as those in traditional print or broadcast media. The court dismissed the case because the plaintiff was not able to prove actual malice. In another case the Civil and Commercial Court of Appeals ruled against a petition by a dental services company requesting Google to block negative comments against the organization.

Internet Freedom

There were no generalized restrictions on access to the internet or credible reports that the government monitored e-mail or internet chat rooms without appropriate legal authority. Individuals and groups could engage in the expression of views via the internet, including by e-mail and social networks. The International Telecommunication Union reported that 56 percent of individuals in the country used the internet during the year.

Academic Freedom and Cultural Events

There were no government restrictions on academic freedom or cultural events.

b. Freedom of Peaceful Assembly and Association

The constitution provides for freedom of assembly and association, and the government generally respected these rights.

c. Freedom of Religion

See the Department of State's *International Religious Freedom Report* at www.state.gov/j/drl/irf/rpt.

d. Freedom of Movement, Internally Displaced Persons, Protection of Refugees, and Stateless Persons

The constitution provides for freedom of internal movement, foreign travel, emigration, and repatriation, and the government generally respected these rights.

The government cooperated with the Office of the UN High Commissioner for Refugees (UNHCR) and other humanitarian organizations in providing protection and assistance to refugees, asylum seekers, and other persons of concern. According to the UNHCR, as of January there were 3,488 refugees and 1,921 asylum seekers residing in the country.

Protection of Refugees

Access to Asylum: Laws provide for the granting of refugee status, and the government has established a system for providing protection to refugees.

Statistics were not available on the number of individuals to whom the National Committee for Refugees granted refugee status, the number of asylum cases pending, or the total number of petitions filed during the year. Decisions on asylum petitions may take up to two years to adjudicate.

Section 3. Respect for Political Rights: The Right of Citizens to Change Their Government

The constitution provides citizens the right to change their government peacefully, and citizens exercised this right through periodic, free, and fair elections based on universal suffrage.

Elections and Political Participation

Recent Elections: In October 2011 voters re-elected President Cristina Fernandez de Kirchner of the Front for Victory coalition in polling described by media and various NGOs as free and fair. The country held legislative midterm elections on October 27. Voters elected one-half of the members of the Chamber of Deputies, representing all 23 provinces and the city of Buenos Aires, and one-third of those in the Senate, representing eight provinces. Local observers considered these elections generally free and fair.

Following 2012 legislation on voting rights, voters ages 16 and17 were added to the electoral register for the first time and participated in the August primary elections.

Participation of Women and Minorities: Regulations provide that at least one-third of the candidates on election slates for both houses of congress must be women. There were 28 women in the 72-seat Senate and 90 women in the 257-seat Chamber of Deputies. The president, two of the seven Supreme Court justices, and two cabinet ministers were women. (A third woman cabinet minister moved to a diplomatic post in May.) No known ethnic or racial minorities were in the national legislature. There were no known indigenous, ethnic, or racial minorities in the cabinet or on the Supreme Court.

Section 4. Corruption and Lack of Transparency in Government

The law provides criminal penalties for corruption by officials; however, multiple reports alleged that executive, legislative, and judicial officials engaged in corrupt practices with impunity, suggesting a failure to implement the law effectively.

Weak institutions and an often ineffective and politicized judicial system undermined systematic attempts to curb corruption.

Corruption: Cases of corruption occurred in some security forces. The most frequent abuses included extortion of, and protection for, those involved in drug trafficking and prostitution.

On September 3, a federal court in Cordoba Province imposed a six-month suspended sentence on former transportation secretary Ricardo Jaime for concealing documents connected with a judicial investigation for illicit enrichment. In June a judge in Misiones Province indicted police commissioner Hector Ojeda, the then head of the Investigations Unit in Iguazu Falls and one of Governor Closs' bodyguards, for alleged involvement in the robberies of supermarkets and a financial company. Ojeda was under investigation for allegedly covering up the activities of drug traffickers and criminals in the tri-border area.

Allegations of corruption in provincial as well as in federal courts remained frequent.

Vice President Amado Boudou remained under investigation for illicit enrichment and for using his former position as minister of economy to benefit the Old Fund Company, a firm in which he had a financial interest. Although Federal Judge Ariel Lijo rejected Boudou's request to throw out the case in August, Cassation Court Judge Javier De Luca ruled in November that courts must immediately assess the evidence in order to continue the case. Additionally Federal Judge Norberto Oyarbide was investigating Boudou in connection with funds that disappeared during Boudou's administration of the country's social security administration.

On June 14, a court convicted former president Carlos Menem and former defense minister Oscar Camilion of arms smuggling to Ecuador and Croatia and sentenced them to five to seven years' imprisonment. Menem also was indicted for his alleged responsibility in the 1995 explosion in a military factory in Rio Tercero, Cordoba Province, which resulted in seven deaths and 300 persons injured. As a senator, Menem holds immunity.

The case charging that former president Fernando de la Rua and senior members of his cabinet bribed national senators in 2000 to vote for the amendment of a labor law continued at year's end.

Whistleblower Protection: Criminal code provisions oblige public officials to file complaints if they witness irregularities. Public employment laws protect officials from termination of employment in such cases but do not cover other forms of retaliation. Cases of corruption can be anonymously reported to the Anticorruption Office of the Ministry of Justice and Human Rights.

Financial Disclosure: Public officials are subject to financial disclosure laws, and the Ministry of Justice's Anti-Corruption Office (ACO) is responsible for analyzing and investigating federal executive branch officials based on their financial disclosure forms. Laws provide for public disclosure, but not all agencies complied, and enforcement remained a problem, since authorities did not sanction public officials for noncompliance. The ACO is also responsible for investigating corruption within the federal executive branch or in matters involving federal funds, except for funds transferred to the provinces. As part of the executive branch, the ACO does not have authority to prosecute cases independently, but it can refer cases to other agencies or serve as the plaintiff and request a judge to initiate a case.

Public Access to Information: While the country does not have a law that provides for public access to government information, a presidential decree provides for access to public documents and information that fall within the jurisdiction of the executive. In August the Supreme Court ordered judges' affidavits to be posted on the Supreme Court's website. A September report by a local NGO reported continuing arbitrary rejections of requests for information, allegedly violating the Habeas Data Law, which specifically provides public access to judicial records and reports of judges' personal assets.

Section 5. Governmental Attitude Regarding International and Nongovernmental Investigation of Alleged Violations of Human Rights

A wide variety of domestic and international human rights groups generally operated without government restriction, investigating and publishing their findings on human rights cases. Government officials usually were cooperative and generally responsive to their views.

Government Human Rights Bodies: The government has a Human Rights Secretariat. Its main objective is to collaborate with the Ministry of Justice, Security and Human rights to promote policies, plans, and programs for the protection of human rights. During the year it published leaflets and books on a range of human rights topics.

In June Prosecutor General Alejandra Gils-Carbo inaugurated the Office of Crimes Against Humanity, charged with investigating and documenting human rights violations that occurred under the military dictatorship of 1976-83.

In July the Ministry of Economy and Public Finance created the Commission for Memory, Truth and Justice to compile information about the workers of the ministry who were persecuted, detained, kidnapped, disappeared, or killed during the military dictatorship.

Section 6. Discrimination, Societal Abuses, and Trafficking in Persons

The law prohibits discrimination based on race, gender, sexual orientation, disability, language, or social status, and the government generally enforced these prohibitions.

Women

Rape and Domestic Violence: Rape, including spousal rape, is a crime, but evidentiary requirements, either in the form of clear physical injury or the testimony of a witness, often presented difficulties in prosecuting such crimes. The penalties for rape range from six months' to 20 years' imprisonment. There were no reports of police or judicial reluctance to act on rape cases; however, women's rights advocates claimed that attitudes of police, hospitals, and courts toward survivors of sexual violence sometimes revictimized the individual.

No statistics were available on the number of rape cases reported during the year. Many rapes went unreported due to fear of further violence, retribution, and social stigma.

The law prohibits domestic violence, including spousal abuse, and complaints are addressed in civil courts to secure protection measures. Family court judges have the right to bar a perpetrator from a victim's home or workplace. The law requires the state to open a criminal investigation potentially resulting in life imprisonment in cases where violence results in death. In November 2012 Congress passed the Femicide Law, imposing stricter penalties on those who kill their spouses, partners, or children as a consequence of gender violence. In July the executive branch enacted a law creating a national DNA registry of sex criminals. According to local NGOs, lack of police and judicial vigilance often led to a lack of protection for victims.

Domestic violence against women was a problem. The civil society organization La Casa del Encuentro reported that 209 women died between January and September as a result of domestic or gender-based violence. Approximately half of these cases occurred in the provinces of Buenos Aires, Cordoba, and Santa Fe. Of these killings, 68 percent involved a husband, boyfriend, or former boyfriend. In at least 20 cases, the woman had filed a complaint against the aggressor for domestic violence.

The Supreme Court's Office of Domestic Violence provided around-the-clock protection and resources to victims of domestic violence. The office received approximately 830 cases of domestic violence each month in the city of Buenos Aires, an estimated 64 percent of which involved violence against women. The office also carried out risk assessments necessary to obtain a restraining order. The "Victims against Violence Program," which operated in the city of Buenos Aires and Chaco Province, empowers a team of specialists from the Justice and Security Ministry to assist victims of domestic violence. The program reported an average of 700 telephone calls per month.

Since 2008 there have been 1,236 reported cases of femicide. Since the highly publicized murder of Wanda Taddei, who was burned to death by her husband in 2010, there have been 66 similar killings, including seven in the first half of the year.

The Ministry of Social Development of the province of Buenos Aires reported 221 formal complaints of physical abuse against women during the first three months of the year. Individuals ages 20 to30 constituted a majority of the victims, and 53 percent of the cases involved psychological and emotional mistreatment.

Pursuant to an October 2012 agreement, the Office of Domestic Violence and the Security Ministry trained members of the Federal Police, Navy, and Gendarmerie in the city of Buenos Aires on domestic violence intervention. Statistics on the number trained were not available at the end of the year.

Public and private institutions offered prevention programs and provided support and treatment for abused women. The Buenos Aires Municipal Government operated a small shelter for battered women.

Sexual Harassment: The law prohibits sexual harassment in the public sector and imposes disciplinary or corrective measures. In some jurisdictions, such as Buenos Aires City, sexual harassment may lead to the abuser's dismissal, whereas in others, such as Santa Fe Province, the maximum penalty is five days in prison.

Reproductive Rights: Couples and individuals generally had the right to decide freely the number, spacing, and timing of children and had the information and means to do so free from discrimination, coercion, and violence. Access to information on contraception and skilled attendance at delivery and in postpartum care were widely available. The law requires the government to provide free contraceptives, and an estimated 64 to70 percent of women used modern contraceptive means.

Discrimination: Although women enjoyed equal rights under the law, including property rights, they continued to face economic discrimination and held a disproportionately high number of lower-paying jobs. Women also held significantly fewer executive positions in the private sector than men, according to several studies. Although equal payment for equal work is constitutionally mandated, the 2013 Global Gender Gap Report estimated that women earned approximately 58 percent as much as men for similar or equal work.

The Supreme Court's Office of Women trains judges, secretaries, and clerks to deal with court cases related to women's issues; it also seeks to ensure equal access for women to positions in the court system. The office also trained judges, prosecutors, judicial staff, and law enforcement agents to increase awareness of gender-related crimes and develop techniques to deal with gender-related cases and victims.

Children

Birth Registration: The country provided universal birth registration, and citizenship was derived both by birth within the country's territory and from one's parents. Parents have 40 days to register births, and the state has an additional 20 days to do so. The Ministry of Interior may issue birth certificates to children under age 12 whose births were not previously registered.

Child Abuse: Child abuse was common; for example, the Office of Domestic Violence reported that 30 percent of the cases it received per month involved children.

Forced and Early Marriage: The legal minimum age of marriage for men and women is 18.

Sexual Exploitation of Children: Sexual exploitation of children, including in prostitution, was a problem. The minimum age of consensual sex is 18. There is a statutory rape law with penalties ranging from six months to 15 years in prison, depending on the age of the victim. Additionally, regardless of age, if a judge finds evidence of deception, violence, threats, abuse of authority, or any other form of intimidation or coercion resulting in sexual intercourse, the minimum sentence increases to six years. Several prominent cases of child sexual abuse were reported during the year. During the first half of the year, the Ministry of Justice program Victims against Violence assisted 329 minors who were victims of sexual abuse.

The law prohibits the production and distribution of child pornography with penalties ranging from six months to four years in prison. While the law does not prohibit the possession of child pornography by individuals for personal use, it provides penalties ranging from four months to two years in prison for possession of child pornography with the intent to distribute it. Additionally the law provides penalties ranging from one month to three years in prison for facilitating access to pornographic shows or materials to minors under the age of 14.

During the year prosecutors and police pursued cases of internet child pornography. In August Federal Police arrested 30 individuals for producing and distributing child pornography online. They discovered 1,500 CDs, computers, and external disks with pornographic material.

On July 30, authorities in Cordoba arrested a teacher for distributing child pornography online, charging him with distribution and commercialization of child pornography. After conviction, a court sentenced the individual to two years' imprisonment.

International Child Abductions: The country is a party to the 1980 Hague Convention on the Civil Aspects of International Child Abduction. For information see the Department of State's report on compliance at http://travel.state.gov/abduction/resources/congressreport/congressreport_4308.h tml as well as country-specific information at http://travel.state.gov/abduction/country/country 5875.html.

Anti-Semitism

The Jewish community consisted of approximately 250,000 persons. Sporadic acts of anti-Semitic discrimination and vandalism continued. The Delegation of Argentine Jewish Associations (DAIA) received complaints of anti-Semitism during the year.

The most commonly reported anti-Semitic incidents were virtual slurs posted on various websites, graffiti, verbal slurs, and the desecration of Jewish cemeteries. In 2012 the DAIA received 243 distinct reports of anti-Semitic behavior. The city of Buenos Aires had the most cases filed, and the DAIA claimed cases in the provinces were likely underreported. On March 19, the municipality of General Campos, Entre Rios Province, distributed tax-payment receipts printed with the sentence: "Be a patriot, kill a Jew." The DAIA declared that municipal authorities were responsible for the bill and demanded administrative sanctions and removal from office of the responsible party.

The investigation continued into the 1994 bombing of the Argentina Israelite Mutual Association (AMIA) community center in Buenos Aires that killed 85 persons. The federal prosecutor investigating the case continued to seek the arrest of eight Iranians for their alleged involvement in the bombing. Early in the year the government ratified a memorandum of understanding with Iran to jointly investigate the AMIA case, and the government continued to negotiate with Iran on the specifics of the agreement's implementation. Jewish community representatives and opposition political leaders continued to criticize the government for engaging in an unclearly conditioned political dialogue and expressed concerns that it could undermine the country's existing judicial investigation. Jewish organizations AMIA and DAIA filed suit against the agreement in July, arguing that the accord is unconstitutional.

The Buenos Aires City government partnered with the interfaith organization Bridge Builders and the French Alliance to sponsor a series of monthly film presentations and discussions to promote religious understanding.

Trafficking in Persons

See the Department of State's *Trafficking in Persons Report* at www.state.gov/j/tip.

Persons with Disabilities

The constitution and laws prohibit discrimination against persons with physical, sensory, intellectual, and mental disabilities in employment, education, air travel and other transportation, access to health care, or the provision of other state services. A specific law also mandates access to buildings by persons with disabilities. While the federal government has protective laws, many provinces have not adopted the laws and have no mechanisms to ensure enforcement. An employment quota law reserves 4 percent of federal government jobs for persons with disabilities, but NGOs and advocacy groups claimed the quota often was not respected.

According to the Ministry of Labor, Employment, and Social Security, more than 12,000 persons with disabilities had obtained jobs through the ministry's programs in the city of Buenos Aires as of May 2011. The programs included various benefits for workers with disabilities, such as free job training programs.

A pattern of inadequate facilities and poor conditions continued in some mental institutions. For example, a press report from April addressed deficient infrastructure and human rights violations in Buen Pastor Psychiatric Hospital in Bell Ville, Cordoba Province. The report described prisoners living in "concentration camp" conditions with open sewers infested with insects and bats' nests in kitchen facilities. Governor De la Sota committed to improving services through increased financial support and advocated to end confinement practices for patients with less severe disabilities.

In early February, following a 2012 request from more than 30 NGOs, the Buenos Aires City education ministry issued regulations to allow children with disabilities to attend schools with their therapists and health-care companions. The effort aimed to promote the inclusion of children with disabilities in schools that also admit children without disabilities. In October three NGOs submitted a report to the UN Committee on the Rights of Persons with Disabilities, sharing concern over discrepancies between domestic legislation and international conventions that guarantee rights to persons with disabilities. The NGOs also claimed Argentina was falling short of compliance with the UN committee's 2012 recommendations to the country.

In August and October, official voting centers for primary and legislative mid-term elections provided special voting tables and braille ballot holders, making the voting process accessible to persons with disabilities.

The National Advisory Committee for the Integration of People with Disabilities under the National Council for Coordination of Social Policies has formal responsibility for actions to accommodate persons with disabilities. The government's actions to improve respect for the rights of persons with disabilities included a program started in September 2012 by Buenos Aires Province that establishes economic incentives for municipalities that hire persons with disabilities as civil servants. The program stipulated that municipalities participating in the program would receive a subsidy payment from the provincial Ministry of Labor.

Indigenous People

The constitution recognizes the ethnic and cultural identities of indigenous people and states that congress shall protect their right to bilingual education, recognize their communities and the communal ownership of their ancestral lands, and allow for their participation in the management of their natural resources. Indigenous people did not fully participate in the management of their lands or natural resources, in part because responsibility for implementing the law is delegated to the 23 provinces, only 11 of which have constitutions recognizing indigenous rights.

Although there is no formal process to recognize indigenous tribes or determine who is an indigenous person, indigenous communities can register with the provincial or federal government as civic associations. A 2010 survey conducted by the National Statistics and Census Institute recorded an indigenous population of more than780,000.

During his visit to the country in late 2011, the UN special rapporteur on the rights of indigenous people, James Anaya, found the "historical exclusion of indigenous peoples is still very apparent," manifested by "the inadequate protection of their rights to their traditional lands, and their continuing marginalization and discrimination." Poverty rates were higher than average in areas with large indigenous populations. Indigenous people had greater than average rates of illiteracy, chronic disease, and unemployment. Indigenous women faced further discrimination based on gender and reduced economic status. The lack of trained teachers hampered government efforts to offer bilingual education opportunities to indigenous people.

The special rapporteur's report indicated indigenous peoples continued to lack adequate participation in decisions affecting their ancestral lands. It added that projects carried out by the agricultural and extractive industries displaced individuals, limited their access to traditional means of livelihood, reduced the area of lands on which they depended, and caused pollution that in some cases endangered the health and welfare of indigenous communities. Local NGOs agreed these findings remained valid during the year.

In May the president of the Social Care Pastoral Committee of the Catholic Church, Bishop Jorge Lozano, expressed concern over the marginalization of indigenous populations throughout the country as exemplified by rates of extreme poverty, illiteracy, and illness. His concerns focused on the Qom community in Formosa Province, and he placed responsibility on the federal and provincial governments.

In May policemen killed a Toba community member in Chaco Province after a violent eviction. Representatives of the Qom Community blamed the Chaco vice governor, Juan Carlos Bacileff Ivanoff, who allegedly ordered the eviction.

Additionally, Abelardo Diaz, son of Qom chief Felix Diaz, was the victim of a violent attack by a group of 30 individuals. Other members of Diaz' family suffered systematic attacks during the year, which local analysts and NGOs attributed to Diaz' repeated demands for formal ownership of Qom land. Formosa provincial authorities minimized the importance of the attacks.

A land survey, initiated by the federal government in 2011, continued during the year. Various NGOs, national deputies, and the Catholic Church claimed the National Institute for Indigenous Rights, the entity charged with surveying land, had mapped only 12 percent of the entire territory despite funding sufficient to make greater progress.

Societal Abuses, Discrimination, and Acts of Violence Based on Sexual Orientation and Gender Identity

Lesbian, gay, bisexual, and transgender organizations operated freely. They worked closely with academic institutions, NGOs, and government authorities without interference.

There was no official discrimination based on sexual orientation in employment, housing, statelessness, or access to education or health care. Overt societal discrimination generally was uncommon, but the National Institute Against Discrimination, Xenophobia, and Racism reported cases of discrimination and police brutality toward the transgender community. In August a transsexual prisoner at Ezeiza Penitentiary reported serious mistreatment by prisoners and penitentiary officials, which two witnesses later confirmed. After the witnesses provided their testimonies, prison guards injured them and confined them to isolation and a psychiatric area.

In April Pedro Robledo was the victim of a violent hate crime at a university party in Buenos Aires. Robledo met with the university president and petitioned for the amendment of the antidiscrimination law to include an article on sexual minorities.

Other Societal Violence or Discrimination

There were no known reports of societal violence against persons with HIV/AIDs, but there were occasional reports of discrimination against persons with the disease. For example, the president of the Argentine Network for People with AIDS reported obstacles for infected individuals to obtain employment. According to the president, medical checkups that diagnose the disease prevent approximately 60 to78 percent of individuals from being hired.

Section 7. Worker Rights

a. Freedom of Association and the Right to Collective Bargaining

With some restrictions, the law provides for the right of all workers to form and join "free and democratic labor unions, recognized by inscription in a special register," conduct legal strikes, and bargain collectively. The law prohibits military and law enforcement personnel from forming and joining unions. The law prohibits discrimination against unions and protects workers from dismissal, suspension, and changes in labor conditions. The law provides for reinstatement for workers fired for union activity.

The law allows unions to register without prior authorization, and registered trade union organizations may engage in certain activities to represent their members, including petitioning the government and employers. The law grants official trade union status to only one union deemed the "most representative" per industrial sector within a specific geographical region. Only unions with such official recognition receive trade union immunity for their officials, are permitted to deduct union dues directly, and may bargain collectively with recourse to conciliation and arbitration. The most representative union bargains on behalf of all workers, and collective agreements cover both union members and nonmembers in the sector. The law requires the Ministry of Labor, Employment, and Social Security to ratify collective bargaining agreements.

The Argentine Workers Central (CTA) and other labor groups not affiliated with the General Confederation of Labor continued to contend that the legal recognition of only one union per sector conflicted with international standards and prevented these unions from obtaining full legal standing. In June the Supreme Court decided a case reaffirming the need for more than one official union per sector and for amendments to the legislation. Congress had not modified labor legislation, however, and the executive branch had not granted such recognition to the CTA by the end of November.

Civil servants and workers in essential services may strike only after a compulsory 15-day conciliation process, and they are subject to the condition that unspecified "minimum services" be rendered. Once the conciliation term expires, civil servants and workers in essential services must give five days' notice to the administrative authority and the public agency that they intend to strike. If "minimum services" were not previously defined in a collective bargaining agreement, all parties then negotiate which minimum services will continue to be provided and a schedule for their provision. The public agency, in turn, must provide clients two days' notice of the impending strike.

The government effectively enforced these laws. Under the law complaints for unfair labor practices can be brought before the judiciary. They may result in a fine being imposed on the employer, or the relevant employers' association where appropriate. There were few cases of significant delays or appeals in the collective bargaining process.

Workers exercised freedom of association and employers respected the right to collectively bargain and to strike. Labor organizations operated independently of government and political parties.

b. Prohibition of Forced or Compulsory Labor

The law prohibits all forms of forced or compulsory labor, and the government generally enforced such laws. Penalties for violations range from four to 15 years in prison and are comparable to other serious offenses. The Ministry of Security and the National Program of Rescue and Accompaniment of Victims under the Ministry of Justice and Human Rights reported rescuing 284 potential victims of forced labor from January through June. The labor ministry carried out several inspections during the year and found various irregularities and potential cases of forced labor. Holding perpetrators accountable and providing victims with services continued to be a problem.

Forced labor occurred. Employers subjected a significant number of Bolivians, Paraguayans, and Peruvians, as well as Argentine citizens from poorer northern provinces, to forced labor in sweatshops, agriculture, and domestic work. Men, women, and children (see section 7.c.) were all victims of forced labor, although victims' gender and age varied by employment sector.

In June the Airport Security Police detained a Colombian citizen on charges of leading an international forced-labor network. The police identified more than 202 Colombians recruited through misleading job offers who were potential victims of forced labor.

In September police agents arrested 10 individuals allegedly participating in an international labor-trafficking network. The network offered attractive jobs in Argentina to Chinese citizens, who travelled to Buenos Aires via Paraguay.

Traffickers sold the victims to Chinese supermarkets, where they worked more than 12 hours a day in deplorable conditions.

Also see the Department of State's *Trafficking in Persons Report* at www.state.gov/j/tip.

c. Prohibition of Child Labor and Minimum Age for Employment

The minimum age for employment is 16. In rare cases labor authorities may authorize a younger child to work as part of a family unit. Children between the ages of 16 and 18 may work in a limited number of job categories and for limited hours if they have completed compulsory schooling, which normally ends at age 18. Children under 18 cannot be hired to perform perilous, arduous, or unhealthy jobs. The law requires employers to provide adequate care for workers' children during work hours to discourage child labor.

Provincial governments and the city government of Buenos Aires are responsible for labor law enforcement. Legal penalties for employing underage workers range from 1,000 to 5,000 pesos ($200 to $1,000) for each child employed. Subsequent violations may lead the labor authority to close the company for up to 10 days, and the company is then prevented from becoming a vendor to the government for a year. On March 20, the Senate unanimously passed a law punishing child labor with penalties ranging from one to four years' imprisonment, unless the crime falls under a more serious category. The law excludes parents. These penalties are sufficient to deter violations.

While the government enforced applicable laws, observers noted that inspectors often were well connected to the subjects of inspection and that corruption remained an obstacle to compliance, especially in the provinces.

Child labor occurred. According to a 2004 government survey, an estimated 450,000 children worked, amounting to 7 percent of children between the ages of five and 13 and 20 percent of children over the age of 14. Employing preliminary data from the corresponding 2012 survey, the Ministry of Labor reported a 66 percent decline in child labor rates between 2004 and 2012. In rural areas children worked on family and third-party farms producing such goods as blueberries, cotton, garlic, grapes, olives, strawberries, tobacco, tomatoes, and yerba mate. Children working in the agriculture sector often handled pesticides without proper protection. In urban areas some children engaged in domestic service and worked on the street selling goods, shining shoes, and recycling trash. According to government sources, some children worked in the manufacturing sector producing such goods as bricks, matches, fireworks, and garments. Children also worked in the mining, fishing, and construction sectors. Officials noted reports of children forced to work as street vendors and beggars in the capital. Commercial sexual exploitation of children occurred as well (see section 6, Children).

Also see the Department of Labor's *Findings on the Worst Forms of Child Labor* at www.dol.gov/ilab/programs/ocft/tda.htm.

d. Acceptable Conditions of Work

In August the government increased the monthly minimum wage for most workers to 3,300 pesos ($660). The National Census and Statistics Institute estimated a family of four needed 1,708 pesos ($342) to remain above the poverty line.

Federal law sets standards in the areas of health, safety, and hours. The maximum workday is eight hours, and the maximum workweek is 48 hours. Overtime pay is required for hours worked in excess of these limits. The law sets minimums for periods of rest, requiring a minimum of 12 hours of rest prior to the start of a new workday. Sundays are holidays, and those required to work on Sundays are paid double. Labor law mandates a minimum of 14 days and a maximum of 35 days of paid vacation, depending on the length of the worker's service.

The law sets premium pay for overtime, adding an extra 50 percent of the hourly rate on ordinary days and 100 percent on Saturday afternoons, Sundays, and holidays. Employees cannot be forced to work overtime unless work stoppage would risk or cause injury, the need for overtime is caused by an act of God, or other exceptional reasons affecting the national economy or "unusual and unpredictable situations" affecting businesses occur.

The law requires employers to insure their employees against accidents at the workplace and when traveling to and from work. The law requires that employers either provide insurance through a labor risk insurance entity or provide its own insurance to employees to meet specified requirements set forth by the national insurance regulator. In October 2012 Congress amended the Labor Risks Law to increase compensation for workers' death or incapacity, while limiting the workers' entitlement to file a complaint if the workers accept the insurance company's compensation.

In March Congress unanimously approved an amendment to the domestic employee law that expands workers' rights and benefits to domestic employees, rural workers, freelance workers, and the volunteer firemen corps.

Laws governing acceptable conditions of work were not enforced universally, particularly for workers in the informal sector. The Ministry of

Labor, Education, and Social Security has responsibility for enforcing legislation related to working conditions. The ministry continued inspections to ensure companies registered their informal workers. During the year the government increased labor inspections to detect unregistered or compulsory work, mainly in rural areas. During 2011, the most recent year for which data are available, the Labor Ministry reported that it had 479 labor inspectors. Information was unavailable regarding the number of inspections during the year, violations encountered by inspectors, and fines or penalties imposed. According to a 2007 study by the International Labor Organization, 60 percent of employed citizens ages 15 to 24 were engaged in informal labor. The Superintendence of Labor Risks serves as the enforcement agency to monitor compliance of health and safety laws and the activities of the labor risk insurance companies.

Most workers in the formal sector earned significantly more than the minimum wage. In general the minimum wage served to mark the minimum pay an informal worker should get, although formal workers' pay was usually higher.

According to the Labor Risk Superintendency, in 2010, the most recent year for which data were available, there were 61.6 worker fatalities per million workers. Agriculture recorded 184.6 fatalities per million workers, construction 196.7 fatalities per million, and transport 157.2 fatalities per million.

In: Argentina
Editor: Eileen Mckinney
ISBN: 978-1-63482-251-0

Chapter 4

ARGENTINA 2013 INTERNATIONAL RELIGIOUS FREEDOM REPORT*

U.S. Department of State; Bureau of Democracy, Human Rights and Labor

EXECUTIVE SUMMARY

The constitution and other laws and policies protect religious freedom, and in practice, the government generally respected religious freedom.

There were reports of societal discrimination based on religious affiliation, belief, or practice, including reports of anti-Semitism.

U.S. embassy officers regularly discussed religious freedom with community leaders as well as the government. Embassy representatives attended events organized by religious groups that addressed religious freedom and promoted interfaith awareness and appreciation.

Section I. Religious Demography

The U.S. government estimates the total population at 42.6 million (July 2013 estimate). A 2008 study by the National Council of Scientific and

* This is an edited, reformatted and augmented version of a report issued by the U.S. Department of State; Bureau of Democracy, Human Rights and Labor, July 2014.

Technical Research and the National Agency for the Promotion of Science and Technology estimates Roman Catholics constitute 76 percent of the population. Baptists, Jews, Muslims, Jehovah's Witnesses, Lutherans, Methodists, and members of The Church of Jesus Christ of Latter-day Saints (Mormons) each total less than 5 percent of the population. Leaders of diverse religious groups note the recent growth of evangelical Protestant communities. While exact numbers are difficult to confirm (national census data does not track religious affiliation), the Jewish population is approximately 250,000-300,000 and the Muslim population is estimated to be between 400,000 and one million.

Section II. Status of Government Respect for Religious Freedom

Legal/Policy Framework

The constitution and other laws and policies generally protect religious freedom. The constitution grants all residents the right "to profess their faith freely." The law provides the legal framework for religious freedom.

By law, the government "sustains the apostolic Roman Catholic faith" and provides tax-exempt subsidies to the Catholic Church. The Catholic Church receives institutional privileges such as school subsidies, significant autonomy for parochial schools, and licensing preferences for radio frequencies.

The law requires that non-Catholic religious groups register with the Secretariat of Worship as civic (rather than religious) associations and report periodically to maintain their status. To register, the Secretariat of Worship requires religious groups to have a place of worship, an organizational charter, and an ordained clergy. Registration is not required for private religious services, such as those in homes but is necessary for public activities. Registration is also necessary to receive tax-exempt status and to allow foreign missionaries to apply for visas.

Foreign missionaries of registered religious groups need to apply to the Secretariat of Worship, which in turn notifies immigration authorities to request the issuance of the appropriate documents.

Public education is secular; however, students may request instruction in the religion of their choice, which may be conducted in school or at a religious institution. Many churches, synagogues, and mosques operate private schools.

The National Institute against Discrimination, Xenophobia, and Racism (INADI), a government agency under the jurisdiction of the Justice Ministry and whose board includes representatives of the major religious groups, investigates suspected incidents of discrimination based on religion. The agency also supports victims of religious discrimination and promotes proactive measures to prevent discrimination.

The government is a member of the International Holocaust Remembrance Alliance.

Government Practices

The Buenos Aires Directorate General for Religious Affairs and the national Secretariat of Worship sent official representatives to religious freedom conferences, rabbinical ordinations, Rosh Hashanah and Eid al-Fitr celebrations, as well as to religious activities held by Protestant and Orthodox churches.

INADI's religious freedom forum held monthly meetings with leaders across the religious spectrum.

The international investigation of the 1994 bombing of the Jewish Argentine Mutual Aid Association (AMIA) building in Buenos Aires that killed 85 persons continued. The federal prosecutor investigating the case continued to seek the arrest of eight Iranians for their alleged involvement in the bombing. In January the government signed a memorandum of understanding with Iran to jointly investigate the AMIA case. The government began negotiations with Iran on the specifics of its implementation. The Delegation of Argentine Israelite Associations (DAIA) and AMIA have challenged the constitutionality of the agreement.

On March 19, the municipality of General Campos in Entre Rios province disbursed tax payment receipts printed with the phrase "Be a patriot, kill a Jew." DAIA called for administrative sanctions and the responsible individual's removal from office. The mayor of General Campos publicly censured and dismissed the employee immediately.

Section III. Status of Societal Respect for Religious Freedom

There were reports of societal discrimination based on religious affiliation, belief, or practice.

DAIA received 243 complaints of anti-Semitism during 2012, the most recent data available, representing a 7 percent decrease compared to 2011. The most commonly reported incidents were anti-Semitic messages posted on websites, anti-Semitic graffiti, verbal slurs, and other forms of harassment.

Local press reported five cases of vandalism occurring in two Methodist churches and three Catholic places of worship. The first incident occurred during a student led demonstration in September when a group of individuals broke into a local Catholic cathedral, vandalized it and set the structure on fire. A wide range of political and religious leaders attended a public mass to express their condemnation of the incident. On November 9, vandals attacked a Methodist Church and destroyed relics of significant historical value.

On November 12, a Catholic protest group interrupted an interfaith ceremony commemorating Kristallnacht at the Metropolitan Cathedral of Buenos Aires. Local Jewish organizations and the Catholic Archbishop of Buenos Aires denounced the protestors.

On July 29, swastikas were found painted in the Republic of the Children Park in La Plata, Province of Buenos Aires.

Leaders of the Jewish, Muslim, and various Christian communities publicly welcomed the election of Cardinal Jorge Bergoglio as Pope.

Section IV. U.S. Government Policy

U.S embassy representatives met periodically with religious leaders to discuss religious freedom and incidents of religious discrimination. In meetings with government officials, embassy staff discussed the status of the AMIA case as well as government efforts to advance religious freedom.

Embassy representatives attended events organized by religious groups and nongovernmental organizations that addressed religious freedom and promoted interfaith awareness and appreciation. One example was the Islamic Center of Argentina's Feast of Sacrifice celebration held annually at the Ministry of Foreign Affairs.

In: Argentina
Editor: Eileen Mckinney

ISBN: 978-1-63482-251-0

Chapter 5

2014 INVESTMENT CLIMATE STATEMENT: ARGENTINA*

Bureau of Economic and Business Affairs

EXECUTIVE SUMMARY

The Government of Argentina (GOA) took actions in the past year to improve the investment climate in Argentina. To regain investor confidence, the GOA settled outstanding international arbitral awards, engaged with the International Monetary Fund (IMF) to improve economic reporting data, and compensated the Spanish-firm Repsol for the partial expropriation of YPF in 2012. Argentina also engaged with the Paris Club group of creditors to address legacy debt issues. A January 2014 currency devaluation reduced costs and asset prices in dollar terms.

Over the past year, one measure of Argentina's country risk has fallen approximately 35 percent from 1210 basis points to 790. The GOA has signaled its desire to see continued foreign direct investment (FDI) flows to enhance the nation's productive capacity and GDP growth potential. Although improved from the year before, investor confidence remains low. Longstanding concerns regarding the lack of transparency in government policymaking diminish the attractiveness of prospective investments in some sectors. Decisions that affect companies, both foreign and domestic, are

* This is an edited, reformatted and augmented version of a report issued by the U.S. Department of State, June 2014.

frequently taken without industry input and rarely with a formal comment period. GOA actions to curb the remittance of profits abroad have also led some foreign companies to question whether their money should be invested in the country if they are unable to access it later. Currency controls delay companies' access to dollars to pay suppliers.

The GOA's all-encompassing import licensing system has made it burdensome to import the materials necessary for the day-to-day functioning of a business. Factories and distributors occasionally sit idle while the GOA delays granting approval to move inputs through customs, a process that can be unpredictable. Companies that export more from Argentina than they import generally receive preferential access, but even these firms have reported difficulties in securing certain goods. Price controls have also caused difficulties for businesses.

Argentina continues to owe debt to private bondholders. Ninety-two percent of the defaulted USD 82 billion of private debt has been swapped for a mix of new bonds with a substantial loss in net present value. Some bondholders, known as the "holdouts," have not participated in the swaps and continue to pressure Argentina via the U.S. courts to settle its outstanding debt for the actual amount they are owed plus interest.

Argentina's growth slowed in 2013 to 3 percent and unemployment remained steady at 6.4 percent, according to official figures. Central Bank reserves dipped to USD 27 billion down from their high of USD 52 billion in early 2011. This decline has been due to reserves having been used to service debt, maintain the exchange rate, and meet other balance of payment needs. The 2014 budget allowed the use of USD 9.8 billion in Central Bank reserves to make debt payments. Argentina ran current and financial account deficits in 2013 that also contributed to a decline in reserves.

After several years of publishing non-credible statistics, Argentina's official statistics agency (INDEC) released substantially revised inflation and GDP growth data that are closer in line with private estimates. The IMF had formally censured Argentina in February 2013 because of manipulation of inflation and GDP data, a breach of obligation to the Fund under the Articles of Agreement. As of publication of this report, the IMF had not yet released its conclusions regarding its review of Argentina's new data.

1. Openness to, and Restrictions Upon, Foreign Investment

According to a Presidential decree governing foreign investment in Argentina, foreign companies may invest in Argentina without registration or prior government approval, and on the same terms as investors domiciled in Argentina. Investors are free to enter Argentina through merger, acquisition, green-field investments, or joint ventures. Foreign firms may also participate in publicly-financed research and development programs on a national treatment basis.

In December 2011, the Argentine Congress passed Law 26.737 (Regime for Protection of National Domain over Ownership, Possession or Tenure of Rural Land) limiting foreign ownership of rural land to a maximum of 15 percent of all national productive land. Individuals or companies from a same nation may not hold over 30 percent of that amount; and individually each foreign individual or company faces an ownership cap of 1,000 hectares (2,470 acres) in the most productive farming areas, or the equivalent in terms of productivity levels in other areas. As approved, the law is not retroactive. Section 11 of the Law establishes that "for the purposes of this Law and according to the Bilateral Investment Treaties (BITs) underwritten by the Republic of Argentina that are in force at the time this Law becomes valid, the acquisition of rural land shall not be considered an investment as it is a non-renewable natural resource provided by the host country."

Foreign and Argentine firms generally face the same tax liabilities. In general, taxes are assessed on consumption, imports and exports, assets, financial transactions, and property and payroll (social security and related benefits).

The GOA has established a number of investment promotion programs. Those programs allow for Value-Added Tax (VAT) refunds and accelerated depreciation of capital goods for investors and offer tariff incentives for local production of capital goods. They also include sectoral programs, free trade zones, and a Special Customs Area in Tierra del Fuego Province, among other benefits. A complete description of the scope and scale of Argentina's investment promotion programs and regimes can be found at http://www.industria.gov.ar, http://www.inversiones.gov.ar and http://www.mecon.gov.ar/basehome/promocion.htm. Information about programs that specifically apply to small and medium businesses may be found at http://www.sepyme.gov.ar.

Argentina

Measure	Year	Index or Rank	Website Address
TI Corruption Perceptions Index	2013	(106 of 177)	http://cpi.transparency.org/cpi2013/results/
Heritage Foundation's Economic Freedom Index	2013	(166 of 178)	http://www.heritage.org/index/ranking
World Bank's Doing Business Report "Ease of Doing Business"	2013	(126 of 189)	http://doingbusiness.org/rankings
Global Innovation Index	2013	(56 of 142)	http://www.globalinnovationindex.org/content.aspx?page=gii-full-report-2013#pdfopener

2. Conversion and Transfer Policies

The GOA began imposing significant restrictions on remittances of capital overseas in 2011. These were formally implemented in December 2012 with Resolution 3417. In 2012, the Central Bank issued Regulation A-5318 officially banning the purchase of dollars by residents (either Argentine or foreign) as a form of financial savings (although it does not prevent residents from maintaining existing dollar saving accounts and time deposits). This measure formally ended the previous norm that had allowed individuals to buy up to USD 2 million per month without having to specify the destination of the funds (e.g., debt payment, investments, savings, international travel expenses, etc). Residents could only buy foreign currency for international tourism purposes, and these purchases were also subject to caps and controls by the GOA of the origin of funds to acquire the currency and a 35 percent withholding tax that can be deducted from an individual's income and wealth tax obligation The Federal Tax Authority (AFIP) subsequently uses Resolution 3333 to regulate retail purchases of foreign exchange for travel. Requestors provide information as to the source of their money and proof that it was acquired legally. In addition to other personal data such as birth date, profession, and tax ID numbers, they must also provide details about their planned trips, including where, when, and why they are traveling. Since the issuance of this norm, the government has reportedly provided additional verbal instruction to banks and foreign exchange houses that further limit the purchase of foreign exchange.

In January 2014, the GOA allowed residents to purchase a limited quantity of foreign exchange for savings depending on the person's declared income. The buyer can choose withdraw the foreign currency within the first year and pay a 20 percent tax, or else leave the funds in a local bank for a year longer with no tax.

Since 2011, government restrictions on foreign currency purchases have led to the expansion of an informal retail foreign exchange market. The informal dollar rate reached ARS 13 to the USD in January 2014, exceeding the official exchange rate (ARS 8 pesos to the USD) by more than 60 percent. As of publication, the gap between the informal and the official exchange rate has fallen to 30 percent.

Companies have reported difficulties in exchanging pesos for dollars in order to pay for imports. These measures are thought to be in place to address balance of payments concerns, but they have resulted in occasional goods shortages and difficulties for companies doing business in Argentina. Companies must complete multiple steps to import a good into the country. Certificates-of-origin for some goods must be notarized by the Argentine embassy or consulate in the country in which they were produced. This consularization requirement holds for products that have multiple parts from multiple countries. The company must then obtain import license approval, which is known by its Spanish-language acronym "DJAI." Following DJAI approval, companies must then petition the Central Bank for access to foreign exchange. Companies are also often asked to submit detailed financial and operational information.

The GOA subjects speculative capital inflows to three major requirements: (a) investments may not be transferred out of the country for 365 days after their entry; (b) proceeds from foreign exchange transactions involving these investments must be paid into an account in the local financial system; and (c) a 30 percent unremunerated reserve requirement, meaning 30 percent of such transactions must be deposited in a local financial entity for 365 days in an account that is denominated in dollars and receives no interest payment.

There are some notable exceptions to the deposit requirement. A deposit is not required for capital inflows to finance energy infrastructure. Nor is a deposit required on inflows for the purchase of real property by foreigners as long as the foreign exchange liquidation occurs on the day of settlement (and transfer of the title). A deposit is also not required for inflows from foreigners to be used for (a) tax payment and (b) social security contributions within 10 days of the settlement of the foreign currency. In October 2011, the Central Bank imposed new market controls on non-residents. They are now required to immediately "register capital inflows into the local foreign exchange market when they purchase a local company, contribute capital, or purchase real estate."

Foreign entities are banned from participating in Central Bank initial bond offerings, but foreign firms may trade Central Bank debt instruments on the secondary market. The Central Bank also requires that exporters deposit U.S. dollar proceeds from exports in "local" banks (cuentas de corresponsalía de entidades financieras locales) within a specified number of days depending on the good exported (usually between 10-30 days).

Hard currency earnings on exports, both from goods and services, must be converted to pesos in the local foreign exchange market. In 2011, the GOA eliminated the exceptions previously granted to hydrocarbon and mining exports. These firms must now convert their revenues to pesos on the local foreign exchange market. Revenues from re-exports of some temporary imports and exports to Argentine foreign trade zones are still exempted from this requirement.

In October 2011, the Argentine insurance regulator issued Resolution 36.162 requiring "all investments and cash equivalents held by locally registered insurance companies be located in Argentina." This has exposed insurance companies to greater country risk since they are unable to diversify their assets outside of Argentina. In 2012, the GOA further expanded the investment requirements for insurance companies requiring them to allocate part of their overall investments in "instruments related to local productive projects." The minimum percentage required ranges from 5 percent for labor risk insurers to 10 percent for property insurers and 12 percent for life insurers. A government committee composed of the secretaries of Finance, Economic Policy and Development, Internal Trade, Industry, and SMEs as well as the superintendent of Insurance determine the projects eligible to receive such investments.

The Argentine Central Bank issued Circular A5272/73 in January 2012 increasing bank liquidity requirements for operational risks and minimum capital requirements, which sharply limited dividend payments.

The Central Bank expanded in 2012 the list of activities involving the transfer of money abroad by local subsidiaries to headquarters that will require prior approval (Circular A5295). These activities now include: IT services; business and professional services' royalties, patents, trademarks and copyrights; commercial guarantee payments on exports of goods and services;

foreign film, audio and video rights; and services for technology transfer, and rental and leasing income, among other activities. The regulations apply to transactions greater than USD 100,000 in value.

In February 2014, the Central Bank issued Circular A5536 capping the foreign exchange exposure of private banks. The norm limits a financial institutions' foreign currency exposure to 30 percent of their net worth and future exchange rate contracts to 10 percent. Private estimates suggest that 50 percent of the positions held by banks in Argentina are "dollarized," representing nearly USD 9 billion in assets. This implied that banks will liquidate USD 3.5 billion through a mix of foreign currency, dollar bonds, and future contracts – with most of that presumably going to Argentina's Central Bank.

3. Expropriation and Compensation

Section 17 of the Argentine constitution affirms the right of private property and states that any expropriation must be authorized by law and be previously compensated. Fair compensation for expropriation is also guaranteed by international treaty obligation. Article 4 of the United States-Argentina BIT states that investments shall not be expropriated or nationalized except for public purpose upon prompt payment of the fair-market value in compensation. In October 2008, the government nationalized Argentina's private pension funds, which amounted to approximately one-third of total GDP, and transferred the funds to the government social security agency. In December 2008, the Argentine parliament also passed legislation nationalizing the Spanish- owned flag air carrier Aerolineas Argentinas.

President Cristina Fernandez de Kirchner expropriated 51 percent of oil and gas company YPF from Spanish-owned Repsol in 2012. The state takeover of the company was widely criticized by the European Union and others and increased investor caution. The government announced a settlement with Repsol approximately two years later in 2014, which the Argentine congress approved on April 23, 2014.

4. Dispute Settlement

The GOA officially accepts the principle of international arbitration. The United States- Argentina BIT provides for binding international arbitration of investment disputes that cannot be settled through amicable consultation and negotiation between the parties. The GOA is a member of the International Center for the Settlement of Investment Disputes (ICSID), the United Nations Commission on International Trade Law (UNCITRAL), and the World Bank's Multilateral Investment Guarantee Agency (MIGA). Companies that seek recourse through Argentine courts may not also pursue recourse through international arbitration.

Prior to and following the 2001/2 Argentine economic crisis, a number of U.S. investors in privatized public utilities filed ICSID arbitration claims against the GOA arguing that the government rulings de-linking public utility tariffs to foreign inflation indices and a January 2002 "pesofication" of dollar-denominated contracts were a de facto expropriation of their investments. In addition, some U.S. investors filed ICSID arbitration claims based on disputes with provincial governments over unforeseen changes in tax laws and liabilities. Customs treatment and delays in re-negotiating public utility rate changes also provoked investment disagreements.

A longstanding bilateral concern had been non-payment of three final awards granted to U.S. investors: (1) a September 2007 final ICSID judgment awarding approximately USD 133 million plus interest; (2) a September 2009 final judgment awarding USD 165 million plus interest; and (3) a September 2011 final decision awarding USD 2.8 million with interest. Based on claimant petitions alleging that Argentina failed to act in good faith to recognize as binding, or enforce, an arbitral award, the Government of the United States withdrew Argentina's status as a beneficiary of Generalized System of Preferences (GSP) trade benefits in May 2012. Argentina settled the ICSID judgments in October 2013 with the three U.S. companies by paying them a portion of the judgment through a mixture of bonds.

Domestic investment dispute adjudication is available through local courts or administrative procedures. Many foreign investors prefer to rely on private or international arbitration when those options are available.

5. Performance Requirements and Incentives

Formally, no performance requirements are aimed specifically at foreign investors. Government incentives apply to both foreign and domestic firms.

6. Right to Private Ownership and Establishment

In general terms, foreign investors have the same rights as Argentines to establish and own businesses, or to acquire and dispose of interests in businesses.

The media law caps foreign capital ownership of media outlets at 30 percent; requires a minimum national content of between 60 to 70 percent; requires that all transmission signals be owned totally or partially by the national government; establishes a minimum screen quota for Argentine movies; imposes a 0.5 percent of annual revenue fee on foreign programmers for acquiring Argentine films; requires advertisement transmitted by broadcast channels or national channels be produced locally; dictates that all investment in advertising on a non-national signal be covered by exemptions and reductions to income tax; gives foreign media operations differing tax treatment from local companies; and limits the number of broadcasting licenses (based on geography and market segment) to be held by a single licensee. Measures regarding the limitation of foreign ownership in media outlets are not retroactively applied to existing foreign investments currently covered by BIT provisions of non-discriminatory treatment. The U.S.-Argentina BIT contains such protection for U.S. firms.

7. Protection of Property Rights

Secured interests in property, including mortgages, are recognized and common in Argentina. Such interests can be easily and effectively registered. They also can be readily bought and sold. The government of Argentina adheres to most treaties and international agreements on intellectual property and belongs to the World Intellectual Property Organization and the World Trade Organization (WTO). The Argentine Congress ratified the Uruguay Round agreements, including the provisions on intellectual property in Law 24425 on January 5, 1995. Since 1996, however, Argentina has been on the

Office of the U.S. Trade Representative's intellectual property rights Priority Watch List.

Patents: Patent protection remains a theme of particular importance in Argentina's intellectual property rights regime. Extension of adequate patent protection to pharmaceuticals and genetically modified seeds has been a source of bilateral disagreement. Representatives of U.S. companies with significant interest in patented product sales in Argentina say that the patent issuance process is slow and that the backlog of patent applications remains substantial. The National Intellectual Property Institute (INPI) has taken a number of steps to reduce the backlog, including the implementation of fast-track procedures, and opportunities for companies to prioritize their patent applications before INPI several times over the past years. In April 2002, the United States and Argentina reached an agreement with respect to most of the claims in a WTO dispute brought by the United States with respect to Argentina's implementation of its Trade Related Aspects of Intellectual Property Rights (TRIPS) obligations. New patent legislation implementing part of the April 2002 agreement was passed in December 2003. Several issues remain unresolved, however. The United States and Argentina have agreed to leave these issues within the WTO dispute settlement mechanism for action.

Some U.S. and European pharmaceutical firms have expressed concern that some provisions in the amended legislation limit their ability to protect patented products via the use of judicial injunctions to prevent patent violations. The unlicensed production by Argentine firms of pharmaceuticals whose patent rights are owned by foreign companies is a longstanding concern to foreign pharmaceutical companies. In May 2012, INPI published a joint Resolution (118/2012, 546/2012 and 107/2012) that sets new standards for chemical and pharmaceutical patent applications. The guidelines instruct patent examiners to reject new use, new form, and new formulation patents, and specify a number of other changes to drugs that will no longer be acceptable. Companies have stated that the measures were implemented without sufficient transparency and that they significantly diminish protection of their intellectual property. Copyrights, Trademarks, Trade Secrets, and Semiconductor Chip Layout Design: Although Argentina’s copyright law dates to 1930, it provides a sound legal framework to protect intellectual property such as books, films, music, and software. Piracy of CDs, DVDs, and software is widespread, but declining due in large part to the introduction of online content streaming services. While enforcement continues to be sporadic and pirated products are widely available on the market, the government of Argentina has passed laws designed to allow authorities to mount undercover operations; to flag electronically suspect shipments; to facilitate the seizure and detention of suspect merchandise; and to rotate more frequently customs personnel. The Customs administration in 2006 instituted a voluntary trademark registry and owner notification program. Seizures of imported counterfeit goods have since risen dramatically. Some industry actors have noted that further protection for trademark owners should include the right to demand destruction of fraudulent goods to prevent reentry to the market. The government has decreased the time needed for trademark registration and increased the rate at which trademarks are registered. Many industry observers claim that the trademark law, passed in 1980, provides civil damages that are insufficient to be an effective deterrent. The judiciary is reluctant to impose deterrent penalties such as prison sentences in criminal cases, and it is rare that companies press criminal charges. Argentina has no specific law on trade secrets although penalties for unauthorized revelation of trade secrets are applied to a limited degree under commercial law. Argentina has signed the WIPO Treaty on Integrated Circuits, but has no law dealing specifically with the protection of layout designs and semiconductors.

For additional information about treaty obligations and points of contact at local IP offices, please see WIPO's country profiles at http://www.wipo.int/directory/en/.

Embassy point of contact: María Soledad Iglesias Liste IglesiasS@state.gov

Local attorneys list link: http://argentina.usembassy.gov/legal.html

8. Transparency of Regulatory System

Argentine government authorities, including the Ministries of Economy, Production, and Planning and a number of quasi-independent regulatory entities, have mandates to foster competition and protect consumers. Some international investors have expressed concern about abrupt changes in sector-specific regulatory regimes that in their view increase uncertainty.

In general, national taxation rules do not discriminate against foreigners or foreign firms (e.g., asset taxes are applied to equity possessed by both domestic and foreign entities). Government tax authorities scrutinize tax declarations of foreign corporations operating in Argentina with the intent of curbing the use of offshore shell corporations to shelter profits and assets from taxation. This has led to tax disputes with foreign-owned firms that have structured their operations in a manner they believe to be consistent with

Argentine law, while minimizing total corporate tax obligations to all of the countries in which they operate.

Argentina is a member of the U.N. Conference on Trade and Development's international network of transparent investment procedures. Lomas de Zamora, the second largest province of Buenos Aires offers detailed information on administrative procedures applicable to income generating operations, including the number of steps, name and contact details of the entities and persons in charge of procedures, required documents and conditions, costs, processing time, and legal bases justifying the procedures http://lomasdezamora.eregulations.org/. Two other provinces (Berazategui and VicenteLopez) plan to offer the same information system online by the end of 2014.

9. Efficient Capital Markets and Portfolio Investment

The Argentine Securities and Exchange Commission (Comisión Nacional de Valores - CNV) is the federal agency that regulates securities markets offerings. Securities and accounting standards are transparent and consistent with international norms.

The Argentine Congress approved in November 2012 a new law to amend regulations over the domestic stock market. The bill expands the local capital market, but it also provides for greater regulatory intervention in financial deals and corporate administration of listed companies.

U.S. banks, securities firms, and investment funds are well-represented in Argentina and are dynamic players in local capital markets. In 2003, the government began requiring foreign banks to disclose to the public the nature and extent to which their foreign parent banks guarantee their branches or subsidiaries in Argentina.

The private pension fund system -- consolidated in 1995 -- provided a growing base for capital markets until the 2001-2002 economic and financial crises. Following the government's 2005 debt restructuring, private pension funds once again became significant players in domestic capital markets. The government's nationalization of the private pension funds' assets in November 2008 shut down the funds' investment activities, however. As a result of the nationalization, Argentina's Social Security Agency (ANSES) now holds large equity stakes in domestic and foreign firms trading on the local stock exchange, and has also taken on the private pension funds' holdings of federal and provincial government debt. This nationalization considerably decreased the liquidity and depth of the securities market in Argentina.

Following new provisions introduced in the Central Bank charter reform approved in mid-2012, banks operating in Argentina holding at least 1 percent of total market deposits are required to lend at least 5 percent of their deposits -- approximately ARS 15 billion -- for “productive investments” at an interest rate of 15 percent by December 2012. This interest rate is well below private estimates of inflation. In December 2012, the GOA again required major banks to lend another 5 percent of their deposits (approximately ARS 17 billion) for “productive investments” at similar rates required in the previous program. In June 2013, the GOA for a third time required the largest banks to lend 5 percent of their deposits (approximately ARS 20 billion) for “productive investments” by December 2013. In this instance, the program allowed small and medium sized enterprises (SMEs) to use up to 20 percent of their loans for working capital. Once again in December 2013, the government extended the program under similar terms for a fourth time adding about ARS 20 billion at a rate of 17 percent.

10. Competition from State-owned Enterprises

The Argentine government owns stakes ranging from 1 percent to 31 percent in 46 publically- listed companies through ANSES. U.S. investors also own shares in some of these companies. As part of the ANSES takeover of Argentina’s private pension system in 2008, the government agreed to commit itself to being a passive investor in the companies and limit the exercise of its voting rights to 5 percent, regardless of the percentage of a company it actually owned. In April 2011, the GOA removed the 5 percent cap and moved to increase ANSES’ influence over these companies by nominating members for their boards of directors and exercising influence over issues such as dividend payments.

The Argentine government also owns or participates in companies in the following sectors: Civil commercial aviation, water and sanitation, oil and gas, electricity generation, transport, paper production, banking, railway, shipyard, and aircraft ground handling services.

11. Corporate Social Responsibility

There is an increasing awareness of corporate social responsibility (CSR) among both producers and consumers. Foreign and local enterprises both tend to follow generally accepted CSR principles, such as the OECD Guidelines for Multinational Enterprises. CSR practices are welcomed by beneficiary communities throughout Argentina.

12. Political Violence

Demonstrations are common in metropolitan Buenos Aires and occur in other major cities and rural areas. Protesters on occasion block streets, highways, and major intersections, causing traffic jams and delaying travel. While demonstrations are usually nonviolent, individuals sometimes seek confrontation with the police and vandalize private property. Groups occasionally protest in front of the U.S. Embassy or U.S.-affiliated businesses. Though political violence is always concerning, it is not widely considered a hindrance to the investment climate in Argentina.

13. Corruption

According to the World Bank's worldwide governance indicators, corruption remains an area of concern in Argentina. In the latest Transparency International Corruption Perceptions Index (CPI) that ranks countries and territories by their perceived levels of corruption, Argentina ranked 106 out of 178 countries.

There is a strong regulatory framework for combating corruption, but enforcement is uneven, and a slow-moving judiciary makes rooting out corruption difficult. The law provides criminal penalties for official corruption. Public officials are subject to financial disclosure laws, and the Ministry of Justice's Anti-Corruption Office (ACO) is responsible for analyzing and investigating federal executive branch officials based on their financial disclosure forms. The ACO is also responsible for investigating corruption within the federal executive branch or in matters involving federal funds, except for funds transferred to the provinces. While the ACO does not have authority to independently prosecute cases, it can refer cases to other agencies or serve as the plaintiff and request a judge to initiate a case. Reports *of the activities of the ACO may be found at http://www.antico rr upcion.gov.ar.*

Argentina is a party to the OAS Anti-Corruption Convention and ratified the OECD Anti- Corruption Convention in 2001. Argentina has signed and ratified the UN Convention against Corruption (UNCAC). It is an active participant in UNCAC's Conference of State Parties. It is also an active participant in the Mechanism for Follow-up on the Implementation of the Inter- American Convention against Corruption (MESICIC).

14. Bilateral Investment Treaties (BITs)

The governments of Argentina and the United States signed a BIT in 1991. The agreement was amended, ratified by the Congresses of both countries, and entered into force on October 20, 1994. The Argentina-United States BIT can be found on the following site: http://2001-2009.state.gov/documents/organization/43475.pdf. Argentina does not have a bilateral tax treaty with the United States.

The BIT provides protections against capital movement restrictions, expropriations, and performance requirements; it also establishes a means for the settlement of investment disputes.

The BIT lists sectors in which Argentina maintains exceptions to national treatment for U.S. investors: real estate in border areas, air transportation, shipbuilding, nuclear energy, uranium mining, and fishing. U.S. investors must obtain permission from the Ministry of Defense's Superintendency for Frontiers to invest in non-mining activities in border areas.

Argentina has over 50 BITs currently in force and valid double taxation treaties (DTAs) with Australia, United Kingdom, Denmark, Germany, Belgium, France, Italy, Sweden, Canada, Bolivia, Brazil, Finland, Norway, and the Netherlands. In addition, a number of treaties concerning the exemption of income from international transport are in force. Argentina and Switzerland signed on March 20, 2014 a Tax Information Exchange Agreement (TIEA), which will allow both countries to share information on financial accounts and other assets of their respective taxpayers. The agreement must be ratified by the legislatures in both countries.

15. OPIC and Other Investment Insurance Programs

The GOA signed a comprehensive agreement with the Overseas Private Investment Corporation (OPIC) in 1989. The agreement allows OPIC to insure U.S. investments against risks resulting from expropriation, inconvertibility, war or other conflicts affecting public order. OPIC programs are currently used in Argentina. Argentina is also a member of the World Bank's Multilateral Investment Guarantee Agency (MIGA).

16. Labor

Argentine workers are among the most highly educated in Latin America. Wages in dollar terms have historically been competitive. The peso depreciation in January 2014 reduced the dollar cost of labor in Argentina, making it a more attractive place for investors. Argentina has relatively high social security charges and other labor taxes. As of the fourth quarter of 2013, the unemployment rate was 6.4 percent according to official government statistics. The Ministry of Labor, Employment, and Social Security estimated that 33.5 percent of the urban workforce worked in the informal sector as of the fourth quarter of 2013.

Organized labor plays an active role in labor-management relations and in the Argentine political system. Standoffs between management and union activists do occur, but many managers of foreign companies say that they have good relations with their unions. While negotiations between unions and industry are largely market-driven, they occasionally require mediation by the Ministry of Labor.

Argentine law affords unions the right to negotiate collective bargaining agreements and offers recourse to mediation and arbitration. The Ministry of Labor ratifies collective bargaining agreements, which covered roughly 75 percent of the formally employed work force. There are no special laws or exemptions from regular labor laws in the Foreign Trade Zones (FTZs).

17. Foreign-Trade Zones/Free Ports

Argentina has two types of tax-exempt trading areas: FTZs, which are found throughout the country; and the more comprehensive Special Customs

Area (SCA), which covers all of Tierra del Fuego Province and whose benefits apply only to already established firms.

Argentine law defines an FTZ as a territory outside the "general customs area" (GCA, i.e., the rest of Argentina) where neither the inflows nor outflows of exported final merchandise are subject to tariffs, non-tariff barriers, or other taxes on goods. Goods produced within a FTZ generally cannot be shipped to the GCA unless they are capital goods not produced in the rest of the country. The labor, sanitary, ecological, safety, criminal, and financial regulations within FTZs are the same as those that prevail in the GCA. Foreign firms receive national treatment in FTZs.

Under the current law, the GOA may create one FTZ per province, with certain exceptions. More than one FTZ per province may be allowed in sparsely populated border regions (although this provision has not been fully utilized). Thus far, the GOA has permitted FTZs in many of the 23 Argentine provinces. There are already ten free trade zones in Argentina, according to the AFIP and the Argentine government announced in February 2014 the installation of two new free trade zones in Province of Santa Cruz. The new free trade zones will be located in the cities of Caleta Oliva and Rio Gallegos. The most active FTZ is in La Plata, the capital of Buenos Aires Province.

Merchandise shipped from the GCA to a FTZ may receive export incentive benefits, if applicable, only after the goods are exported from the FTZ to a third country destination. Merchandise shipped from the GCA to a FTZ and later exported to another country is not exempt from export taxes. Any value added in an FTZ or re-export from an FTZ is exempt from export taxes.

Products manufactured in an SCA may enter the GCA free from taxes or tariffs. In addition, the government may enact special regulations that exempt products shipped through an SCA (but not manufactured therein) from all forms of taxation except excise taxes. The SCA program provides benefits for established companies that meet specific production and employment objectives.

The SCA program applies only to Tierra del Fuego Province. The government reduced some SCA benefits in the early 1990s. Some of these benefits were later reestablished at first only for those firms previously established in Tierra del Fuego Province, and later applied to all firms. The SCA program is scheduled to expire at the end of 2023. In late 2006, Economy Ministry Resolution 776 abolished the export tax exemption enjoyed by oil companies operating in Tierra del Fuego Province. The Argentine Congress passed a law in November 2009 establishing value- added tax rates up to 21 percent on cell phones, televisions, digital cameras and other electronic items not produced in the southern Tierra del Fuego foreign trade zone. According to the government, the bill aims to increase government revenue through higher tax collection, and encourage investment in Tierra del Fuego to promote local manufacturing and job growth. Additionally, the law removes certain tax benefits and taxes electronic products between 20.5 percent and 26 percent, which is reduced by two-thirds for electronics produced in Tierra del Fuego. However, the use of non-tariff barriers to effectively mandate the local production of many electronic goods is often the primary reason that foreign firms choose to assemble electronic products in Argentina.

18. Foreign Direct Investment and Foreign Portfolio Investment Statistics

Table 2. Key Macroeconomic data, U.S. FDI in host country/economy

	Host Country Statistical source*		USG or international statistical source		USG or international Source of Data: BEA; IMF; Eurostat; UNCTAD, Other
Economic Data	Year	Amount	Year	Amount	
Host Country Gross Domestic Product (GDP) (Millions U.S. Dollars)	2012	468,301	2012	475,500	INDEC, www.indec.gob.ar http://www.worldbank.org/en/country ((The difference is due to statistical corrections done by INDEC on regular basis.))
Foreign Direct Investment	Host Country Statistical source*		USG or international statistical source		USG or international Source of data: BEA; IMF; Eurostat; UNCTAD, Other
U.S. FDI in partner country (Millions U.S. Dollars, stock positions)	2012	N/A	2012	14,396	(BEA) click selections to reach. On historical-cost basis Bureau of Economic Analysis
Host country's FDI in the United States (Millions U.S.	2012	N/A	2012	209	(BEA) click selections to reach Bureau of Economic Analysis

	Host Country Statistical source*		USG or international statistical source		USG or international Source of Data: BEA; IMF; Eurostat; UNCTAD, Other
Dollars, stock positions)					
Total inbound stock of FDI as % host GDP (calculate)	2012	N/A	2012	3.03%	

Table 3. Sources and Destination of FDI

Instructions: CHOOSE YOUR COUNTRY's Name from IMF website http://cdis.imf.org ((Note: IMF censured Argentina in Feb 2013 for reporting unreliable economic data.)) Argentina did not report data according to cdis.imf.org data table.

In past reports we used UNCTAD data, Source: http://unctadstat.unctad.org/TableViewer/tableView.aspx -- According to the United Nations Conference on Trade and Development (UNCTAD) World Investment Report 2012, the total stock of FDI in Argentina at the end of 2012 was estimated at USD 110.7 billion. The stock of U.S. FDI in Argentina in 2012 was estimated at USD 14.4 billion by the U.S. Bureau of Economic Analysis. In 2012, according to UNCTAD, total FDI inflows were estimated at USD 12.5 billion and outward FDI flows amounted to USD 1.1 billion.

Table 4. Sources of Portfolio Investment Argentina, June 2013

Portfolio Investment Assets								
	Top Five Partners (Millions, US Dollars)							
Total			Equity Securities			Total Debt Securities		
World	21,765	100%	World	12,800	100%	World	8,965	100%
United States	20,427	94%	United States	11,803	92%	United States	8,624	96%
Luxembourg	682	3%	Luxembourg	682	5%	Brazil	294	3%
Brazil	397	2%	Spain	124	1%	Germany	39	0.44%
Spain	124	1%	Brazil	103	1%	Chile	4	0.05%
Germany	40	0.18%	China, P.R Mainland	22	0.17%	Uruguay	3	0.03%

Source: http://cpis.imf.org/

19. Point of Contact at Post

Economic Counselor
U.S. Embassy Buenos Aires Avenida Colombia 4300 (C1425GMN)
Buenos Aires, Argentina
+54-11-5777-4747
ECONBA@state.gov

INDEX

#

A

B

C

D

E

F

G

H

I

J

K

L

P

T

U

V

W